the 10¢
decision

How small change pays off big

Team Guide to Exceptional Service

The 10¢ Decision: How Small Change Pays Off Big

Windy City Publishers
2118 Plum Grove Rd., #349
Rolling Meadows, IL 60008

Published in the United States of America

First Edition: 2019

Library of Congress Control Number:
2019908113

ISBN:
978-1-941478-81-3

The 10¢ Decision™ is a trademark of Laurie Guest.

Prologue

Dear Team Member,

You're ready to evaluate your current level of customer service and improve it. Or maybe you're holding this book because the boss is asking you to read it—or making you. I know it can be challenging to find time for training in how to deliver exceptional service when you are busy learning the tasks of your role. You might be frustrated by the staff turnover around you that causes inconsistent service delivery. Management might keep promising to set time aside for staff customer-service training, but somehow daily demands always take over, and they're forced to break that promise in order to deal with the day-to-day duties that keep the place running.

Are you ready for a painless solution that can positively impact your ability to deliver exceptional customer service and help take your career to the next level?

This book shares the guiding principles of customer service with proven techniques to attract and keep customers. One side is written for team members and starts on the "front side" of the book, the direction you are reading now. But not all of the advice is the same-old, same-old service tips you've seen everywhere. I promise to share some fresh strategies to up your customer-service game to a whole new level—or, at the very least, you'll be reminded to actually implement what you already know. At the end of each chapter are discussion questions that, when answered honestly, can lead to forward movement in your career and take you beyond the basics. But that part is up to you. If you read the book without taking action, the insights won't make any impact on your service level or your bottom line. Taking action is the only thing that creates results.

Prologue

It's the Little Things That Matter

Think about a product or service you were drawn to and consider whether the way it was packaged or presented is what first attracted your attention. I've ordered a flight of martinis because of the tiny, fancy, multi-colored glasses they were served in. My friend ordered a very expensive appetizer in an elite club because the caramelized bacon chunks came with a cotton-candy stick. And, let's be honest, the best reason to order saganaki is because the server lights it on fire tableside and yells, "Opa!" Without that show, it's really just fried cheese. (Not to discount the amazing value of fried cheese.)

My favorite example of how packaging can make a difference revolves around bottled water. We all have little things in life that we're picky about. Me? I'm picky about water. That's right, I am a water connoisseur, which is cheaper than being a wine connoisseur.

As you can imagine, it bugs me when I check into a fancy five-star hotel and they want me to pay FOUR DOLLARS for a regular bottle of water. I mean seriously, for $350 a night, I ought to be getting a foot massage from a Chippendales dancer.

My point is that this water costs very little, and yet they can't throw one my way? Swanky hotel, and all I remember is the $4 bottle of water.

Now, let's pop into another hotel where I stayed. Moderately priced this time. Not fancy. I get to the room, parched and winded. I spot a mini-fridge with a sign that reads "Dear Valued Guest." (I love it that they put *my* last name on the sign.) "Please enjoy a complimentary bottle of water from the refrigerator."

It's likely those bottles of water cost the hotel only about 10¢ each when purchased by the truckload. And even though the quality of the water wasn't anything memorable, by simply delivering it to me differently—in the fridge, and free—my perceived value was considerably higher.

Prologue

So why am I telling you all this? Why am I making a big deal out of a bottle of water? Because most of us in business don't realize that sometimes it's the 10¢ decision that can have the biggest impact.

> **...sometimes it's The 10¢ Decision that can have the biggest impact.**

If you really want to provide exceptional service and keep customers coming back, I suggest focusing on small changes. How small? It can be as simple as better word choices or a little extra add-on. But the key is, it doesn't have to cost your company much more than a dime.

Are You Wondering *Why* Laurie?

What makes me an expert on the topic of customer service? How do I know the right combination of service components to help you make the 10¢ decisions to create the ultimate guest experience? It's because of my real-world entrepreneurial experience that started when I was just 5 years old. I grew up inventing new ideas that led to cash, and that was exciting to me.

What I know to be true about customer service is that many organizations think proper treatment of their clients is common sense and that training isn't an issue. Unfortunately, leaders often believe that if they hire good people, their employees will just *know* how to treat customers. WRONG. The basics must be taught, enforced, and reinforced to create the ultimate customer experience.

In this short, easy-to-read book, I share the insights I have gained in each phase of my working life. During every endeavor, I remained committed to providing great service to every customer/patient/guest I encountered. I've also collected quite a few examples through the years that prove each of my points in a relatable fashion. In each chapter, you'll find a lesson that takes a deeper dive into the attributes that can help you achieve great reviews and success simply by improving your guest encounter points.

Prologue

Here's the Best Part!

I realized while writing this book that there are actually two different audiences who need this content. One is you and your fellow team members, who are asked to deliver great customer service on the frontlines but are not always given formal training in how best to treat customers. There is also your boss, who may need help identifying those small ideas that can make a big impact. The boss could be the business owner, a C-suite member, training director, manager, or anyone in a leadership position. In fact, if your work life is anything like mine was, you have *more than one* boss! To make all of this work, you need an integrated approach. All the boss has to do is flip the book over and read from the other direction. Those chapters speak to their needs and core issues. That's right, two books in one!

Also, it's not a bad idea to flip the book yourself and read the other half. If being a manager is on your list of goals, why not get a leg up by learning about service from that side of the desk now? The other side of the book is filled with great stories and creative ideas that show how small changes can pay off big. You'll discover all sorts of ways to help make the 10¢ decision that could have a big impact on the customer service that you and your team members deliver.

Are you ready to get at it? Let's do this!

Match the E-Zone of Your Buyer:
Finding the Right Energy Level for Every Encounter

The E-Zone: This is the energy that you bring to work all day, every day as part of the overall guest experience. *Do you and the rest of your team come to serve each day with energy and enthusiasm? What vibe is your organization giving to your guests?* Understanding your organization's energy levels and how they impact your guests is critical to providing positive guest encounters.

Thrill of the First Paycheck

Growing up on a farm in northern Illinois was a peaceful, almost perfect life. My dad, Shorty, had a great ability to teach life lessons about how to treat people and how to be a successful entrepreneur. Starting when I was 5, once a year during harvest season Dad would allow me to ride in the combine and help harvest corn. Let me clarify the word "help" in that sentence: It meant sit on the arm of his tractor seat and pretend to steer. When the hopper of grain was full, I would watch it unload into the back end of a large grain truck. Then we would climb up into the cab of the truck and take the corn to the grain elevator, where a series of cool things happened—at least as a child I thought it was cool.

When we arrived, we would roll onto a gigantic scale that weighed the truck. Then Dad would pull forward and position the truck over the top of a large grate. When I got the nod, I was responsible for pushing forward the toggle stick inside the cab, which triggered the truck bed to slowly lift into the air, allowing the corn kernels to pour out and down through the floor grate into the grain elevator system.

As I recall this memory, I can still smell the grain and hear the deafening noise of the kernels pouring out. It sounds exactly like when popcorn kernels are poured out of a bag and into a popper. Can you hear it? Now magnify that sound by at least a thousand times. I can remember looking out the back window of the truck and watching that landslide of grain and knowing that this was "my load."

When the truck was empty, it was weighed again, and that's how they determined the amount of product taken to market and how much it was worth. Then came the best part. They cut a check on the spot for the payment, and Dad would pull up to this little window like he had just ordered a burger. They would hand him a check with my name on it, and they would make a really big deal about how hard I had worked that day. I believed it too! Although now I look back and realize all I did was ride shotgun and push a lever.

Why is this experience so vivid in my mind almost 50 years later? It's because of the energy and enthusiasm from the elevator operator. He could have just cut the check and grunted as he handed it to us. He could have just added to it my dad's account to be settled by mail at the end of the week. Instead, he made a big deal out of the encounter. He had an attitude and words that made a little girl feel like a real business person.

Energy attracts people like moth to light.

Because the elevator operator made a fuss over me, the trip to town became a tradition that we continued until I was too old to sit on the arm of the combine. The elevator didn't make more money because of me. Dad would have taken the grain there anyway. But what the enthusiasm did was change up the day for everyone. Energy attracts people like moths to light. If you can match the right energy to the situation, you have a great experience on your hands.

Adjusting Energy Levels in Communication: Finding the Right E-Zone

You can make a subtle change to your communication skills by evaluating your energy level and adjusting it to match your customer. When you do that, I call it being in the E-Zone. Think about energy like the readout on a heart monitor. There's a range that's acceptable, and you go up and down inside that range based on the situation.

Another contributing factor is your own personality. If you're a "Susie Sunshine," for example, be aware that for some encounters you'll need to tone down your positivity. A friendly, outgoing, high-pitched voice is perceived differently than a neutral, quiet, low-pitched voice is, especially if you're delivering bad news. Finding the balance between what feels natural to you and what's needed in the situation will take practice. Before each interaction, think about the optimal point inside the E-Zone that will get the best results.

The personality and age of the person you are communicating with also plays a role in your tone. Be careful not to make stereotypical assumptions that affect your energy and words. The first time my mother had to use an electric scooter at the grocery store, she was very agitated. All of her other physical and mental attributes—hearing, sight, mental awareness, and ability to communicate—were as sharp as when she was in her 50s. After I helped her get situated on the scooter, the gentleman greeter approached. He pointed to the control panel, and in a voice that was overly sweet, too loud, and purposely slowed to one...syllable...at...a...time, he said to her, "Now, this makes you go forward, this makes you go backward, and this button makes it go beep, beep, beep!" He truly sounded liked he was talking to a 3-year-old. My mother made eye contact with me and shared a thought without using words. You can fill in the blank using your imagination. One could argue that his energy was friendly and he was trying to be helpful, but he was nowhere near the E-Zone my mother required in this moment.

> Be careful not to make stereotypical assumptions that affect your energy and words.

Get Creative with Special Moments

Special occasions require their own special E-Zone level, and while they should be a slam dunk, sometimes businesses fall short. Once while I was browsing in a chain store where everything costs a dollar, I witnessed a perfect example of a missed opportunity to create a special moment for a customer. When I walked in, a 6-year-old boy and his father were at the checkout lane. They had a pile of birthday supplies and a *huge* bouquet of helium balloons in a Superman theme. The boy was busting at the seams and prancing around like he needed a bathroom. But what he really wanted was for someone to know it was his birthday and make a fuss over him. After the total was rung up, the clerk turned, grabbed the balloons from the counter behind her, plunked them down in front of the kid, and in a routine voice said to the father, "That will be $25.19." As the father pulled the bills out of his wallet, the little boy said in a voice that was squeaking from joy, "Hey, guess what: Today's my birthday!" She replied, "Well, happy birthday." She didn't use a mean or sarcastic voice, but she said it in the same monotone voice she used to communicate the total of the bill.

This was the entire encounter, almost word for word. Now, she didn't do anything *wrong*. When she rang up the sale, she smiled and even spoke to the child. But what a missed opportunity. The clerk could have rung a bell and, in an enthusiastic tone, announced over the PA system that Jason Kramer was celebrating his sixth birthday! I think the store owner could have done a cool thing by giving the child a special birthday paper sack and telling him he could have any single item in the entire store that would fit in that bag. While the child went looking for his token gift, they could play a special "happy birthday" song over the speakers, written and recorded for just such an event. This entire offer would cost the store very little, but the family wouldn't think of going anywhere else when it came time to buy next year's birthday supplies. Considering that this community has all of the big-box competitors you can think of, how does a solo shop compete?

The answer is to compete with a level of creativity plus one extra tablespoon of enthusiasm that matches the buyer. Get creative!

My son, Evan, tells a great story about the night he turned 21. He waited until the stroke of midnight and then dashed to the nearest bar to order his first legal drink. This is a milestone in many people's lives. It's society's way of saying, "You are now officially an adult." Of course, no one is ever as excited about our birthdays as we are, but if the seller matches the buyer's enthusiasm, loyalty can be built. Evan approached the bartender and, with great excitement and faster-than-normal speech, said, "I just turned 21 a few minutes ago, and I want to order a drink!" The hardened college-town bartender replied in a monotone-at-midnight cadence, "Good for you. What'll ya have?" Now granted, someone in that town probably turns 21 every day, but the bartender could have met this milestone with a much different, even fun response. He could have yelled out at the top of his lungs, "Evan's here for his first legal drink, people!" The owner of the bar could get creative and do something special for the 21-year-olds who come in within the first hour of their birthday. If Chuck E. Cheese could find a way to fuss over him when he was 5, why can't the bar find a way to do the same thing now?

...if the seller matches the buyer's enthusiasm, loyalty can be built.

Be Aware of Encounters That Require *Less* Enthusiasm

For years in my healthcare position as an ophthalmic technician, part of my job was to check the vision of each patient before the doctor's exam. A majority of our patients suffered from cataracts, macular degeneration, or glaucoma—all eye conditions that can limit vision. Although my role was to be friendly and energetic, it would be an insult to use high-octane energy to say to a low-vision patient, "Mrs. Anderson, can you read the big letter for me on the chart?" (Said with a huge smile, excited voice, and a soprano pitch.) That level of energy does not match the gravity of that encounter. To be in the right E-Zone, I need to be aware of the patient's vision status and say in a gentle, encouraging, lower-pitched voice, "Mrs. Anderson, I know it might be tough, but can you make out any part of the big letter on the screen right now?" Obviously, the patient would experience the second version as a kinder level of engaged service.

Stay Truly Present During the Encounter

One struggle I often see frontline staff dealing with is the ability to stay truly present in the moment when a lot is going on around them and much of the work becomes repetitive over time. Once a person tips into robotic mode, mistakes can happen. For example, a few days after my mother's funeral, my dad asked if I could contact the cardiologist's office and cancel an appointment she had scheduled for the following month. The phone was answered by a delightful front-desk assistant. I explained why we needed to cancel the appointment and she expressed the appropriate heartfelt condolences. It took her several minutes to locate the account and confirm she had the right patient file. I'm not certain if she got distracted during this process or if she just inserted a robotic goodbye, but when it was time to disconnect, she said, "OK, you're all set. When your mother is ready to reschedule, just have her give us a call and we can get her back on the books."

For a moment, I was stunned into silence. What you need to know before you read the rest of this story is that my mom was a jokester with a great sense of humor, and I truly believe that if she could hear this tale, she would be laughing so hard. After a week of grieving, this was the moment when the emotion broke for me. It struck me as funny for some reason, and I couldn't help myself from blurting out to the team member while giggling, "Well, that is going to be kind of tough. [pause] Because *she's dead!*" I said the last word louder than necessary, and with emphasis. I didn't do it to be mean; it just popped out. I'm quite certain that when anyone asks this assistant what mistake she has made in her career that was memorable, that call has to rank in her top 10. Because she stepped out of the moment, she lost the point of the call and kicked into her habitual phrase when an appointment is cancelled. I worked in healthcare for more than 20 years. I totally get it. However, on my end of the phone, it was quite a disconnect and changed my impression of the encounter.

Be Aware of Your Own E-Zone

Awareness of your own E-Zone is just as important as assessing that of your guest. Being fully present in a situation, actively listening, and accurately responding are key. What is the one area where you can best improve your E-Zone? Is it your energy at the start of the day? Are you an engaged listener? Are you fully present in the conversation? Be aware of how your voice tone, pace, pitch, and enthusiasm match each situation. To thrive in the E-Zone, evaluate where you are and be very careful to avoid robotic responses to frequently asked questions.

Robotic responses lead to disengaged service that is often costly to the relationship.

The Big 7 of Service

Being energetic and present isn't always enough, though. Providing great service takes hard work and attention—but it's worth it. First impressions are so important, and you only get one shot at them. "Hello" by itself doesn't cut it! To have a truly professional greeting that gets positive feedback, you need to go beyond the hello and engage your guests.

I'm passionate about the topic of back-to-basics customer service because I've seen firsthand the large number of companies that *believe* they have great service. They even include that phrase in their mission statement. Because many customer-service concepts can be seen as common sense, they assume that everyone on board already *knows* the core fundamentals. However, knowing and *doing* are two different things. The way a building looks, the way the staff appears, and certainly the overall impression factors into the decision to try and buy. After secret shopping at many companies, I realized that what many of us may see as basic was somehow getting lost, either during the training process or in the desire of the staff to consistently deliver good service. Because of that, I started teaching "the Big 7 of Service." As you read, rate yourself on a scale of 1 (low) to 5 (high) on your ability to consistently deliver on each of the Big 7.

1. Make Eye Contact

The foundation of any connection starts with looking directly at the guest with an intention to serve. What do I mean by that? Simply looking at a person is not the same as establishing eye contact. The difference between looking at someone and making a connection alters the degree of engagement. Do you really see the person and acknowledge her or his presence? Even if you are already involved with another guest or on the phone, you can accomplish this task in a way that makes the visitor feel a connection. Give a small wave, a smile with a nod, or hold up your index finger, the universal sign for "I'll be with you in one moment."

2. Smile

A lot of people skip one of the easiest good-service steps: the smile. I think it's missing sometimes because smiling is supposed to be natural and genuine. When you're at work, you may not feel like smiling, for one of many reasons. You're too tired, too stressed, too overworked. You may not want to be there at all, or maybe you're just not committed to the mission of the organization. Excuses don't matter. I remember many times in my career when I didn't want to get up and go to work. Once I arrived, however, I knew it was time to focus on the customer and really put my energy into helping people. If you don't feel like smiling, it's hard to do it. To put it bluntly, they call it work for a reason. Even if you have to force a smile, it will make a big difference in your performance.

Also, whether you believe it or not, a greeting *without* a smile and a greeting *with* a smile sound different. Try it. You can hear the difference in tone, which will make a difference in your customer service.

3. Show Signs of Familiarity

People love to hear their names. Have you ever been a frequent visitor to a business where they not only call you by name, but also know what you want even before you ask? I have multiple vendors like that. My dry-cleaning manager pulls my clothes from the rack as soon as he sees my car pull up. At our favorite Chinese restaurant, the owner usually greets us by calling out our standing order as we take a booth. I like it when friends come to visit my home and they feel comfortable enough to open the fridge and get what they need without asking or hang their coats in the closet as though they live there. A feeling of importance or familiarity makes us feel connected.

4. Get in 'Ready Position'

What does "ready position" look like in your company? Ready position means that you are "at attention" and prepared to perform the necessary tasks of your job, like a catcher in baseball who crouches behind the batter, ready to receive the pitch. When you have to make an adjustment before you are ready to engage with a customer, you could give off a negative first impression.

What does the "not ready" position look like? Here are a few examples. Envision the personal banker I was meeting who had her bare feet resting on her desk while she reclined back in her desk chair. When she saw me appear in her doorway, she greeted me by saying, "Hold on a sec. Let me get my shoes on." Or consider the many times I have experienced side conversations between employees that didn't stop when I appeared. Or how about the receptionist at a doctor's office who was eating a cinnamon bun and licking the frosting off her fingers before she extended a pen to me without washing her hands first. Another example is a flight attendant on one of my recent trips. She held a Starbucks coffee cup in her right hand the entire time we were boarding. It had her name written on the side along with a cute smiley face. A little extra touch of customer service from her Terminal 3 barista. She was attempting to serve passengers with just her left hand and doing a subpar job for sure. I had to squelch my overwhelming desire to inquire in my most sarcastic voice, "Hey, Kaitlin, wouldn't it be easier to hang those coats up using two hands?"

Ready position is a behavior that needs to be given careful attention. As a team, make time to discuss the role that posture and being in the present play in your service, then work to improve your ready position.

5. Offer Real Greetings, Not Robotic Acknowledgments

One of the toughest aspects about greetings is that they need to be short, genuine, and repeatable without sounding like a recording. Years ago, when we still watched movies on rented VHS tapes, I made many trips to Blockbuster. As soon as the door opened, I heard an employee shout, "Helloooo," in a long, drawn-out, fake-sounding voice. They must have been trained to say hello to everybody as quickly as possible. Even if the staff member was in the back of the store, you'd hear them yell out a disingenuous greeting.

What about the people who have a fake sound? They pick up the phone and say, "It's a great day at the Shoe Den!" in an automated voice filled with fake enthusiasm that I don't believe. Speaking of automated, the question "How are you?" should be replaced as well. Depending on your specific industry or service, try a script that gets to the core of the connection. For example, "Good morning, thanks for stopping in. My name is Laurie. Please let me know how I can help you today." When a second guest arrives, change it up a little bit. "Hello, welcome. I'm Laurie, and I'm here to answer any questions you might have." Develop a few of these greetings that feel natural to you and rotate them so they feel genuine. Be real by being *present* in the exchange.

6. Shake Hands (When Appropriate), and Do It Right

I'm not a fan of the handshake in general. I wish our society would change to a special wave that has the cultural meaning of the handshake without the touching. But until that happens, a handshake in many industries is common. Interestingly enough, I've rarely see anyone teach a handshake to adults. Here are what I consider the three essential elements of a professional handshake:

- The right hand of each person should meet at the web skin between the forefinger and thumb.
- Grasp the other person's hand firmly—not with a bone-breaking clench and not like a wet noodle. Also, a man grasping a woman's hand by the very edge of her fingers is now passé.
- Connect, pump the other person's hand two or three times—without pulling him or her toward you—then release.

Simple enough. However, after shaking thousands of hands, I can say from experience that top-of-the line hand-shakers are rare. One question that comes up has to do with who should extend a hand first. The answer can vary according to culture, but in the United States, etiquette says the person with greater authority or age should be the first to reach out. If you're going for a job interview or meeting your in-laws for the first time, wait for them to make the first move.

But what about customers? Research didn't provide me with one right answer. So, in my opinion, what makes sense is to shake hands when it feels natural and right. For your organization, decide whether a handshake is mandatory or should be left up to the individual. I always reach out to my clients with a handshake upon arrival. I greet them with a big smile, say the person's name, and follow my own advice on how to shake.

7. Remember the People You Greet

The final entry on the Big 7 proves to be challenging in large retail situations. I walked into my grocery store, and an employee in produce greeted me with, "Good morning. How are you?" Then about 15 minutes later, I was over in the frozen-foods section, and I saw the same employee again: "Hello. How are you today?" It was as if he had never seen me before. This decreased the value of the hello. If you're going to use it, try to find a little memory technique to tell you that you've already greeted that person. When you see that person again, just smile as you go by. Once you've said hello, try really hard to remember that that particular guest is covered.

How did you do on the Big 7? Although the steps may seem elementary, they're not always easy to implement. But making small changes can lead to big results. If you start paying attention to places where you feel your service has been lacking, I bet you'll find that what's been missing falls somewhere in the Big 7.

Match the E-Zone of Your Buyer

Discussion Questions

How does being in "ready position" with the proper posture and mindset play a role in your service?

How would you rate yourself on voice tone, pace, pitch, and enthusiasm to match each situation?

Do you have a plan in place to celebrate special occasions for your guests?

Are there times when you have become too robotic in your responses to guests?

How did you score on the Big 7 of Service quiz? Did your score surprise you?

Anticipate the Customer's Needs:
Perfect the Art of Proactively Providing Service

Reacting swiftly and professionally to situations with customers is one way to keep service running smoothly. *Do you proactively anticipate your customers' needs? Have you found ways to elevate your service and set you apart from your competitors by being one step ahead of the ask?* For some staff, staying hyper-aware of a customer's needs comes naturally. But for others, learning to know what your guests need before they need it is a competence that must be trained.

Serving Up Satisfaction in the Deli
My first *real* job came in the fall of 1980, when I turned 16. I chose the grocery industry and was hired as a deli-counter clerk. They provided a uniform smock in the ugliest shade of roast beef you have ever seen. It had a zipper up the front and pockets so big you could smuggle a bologna in each one.

I worked Tuesday and Thursday nights from 4 p.m. to close and every other weekend. It was on the weekends that I was in charge during my shift. I had to roll out of bed at 5 a.m. to go make the doughnuts. This required mixing a mysterious powder with the exactly correct measurement of water in a metal bowl that was roughly the size of a clothes basket.

But believe it or not, there was one task that was worse than the opening doughnut-making duty: the closing ritual of salad sealing! At the end of the evening, we had to tightly wrap all the open trays in a messy and time-consuming process. Without fail, every single Thursday night, the same elderly lady would arrive just a few minutes before close. Helen always wore the same hand-knitted

Anticipate the Customer's Needs

white sweater with a Kleenex tucked under the right wrist. She was bent forward at a 61-degree angle and had black cat-eye glasses left over from the 1950s. She always needed a quarter-pound of this and a quarter-pound of that, right after I had sealed the salads. It was always the same size serving of the same salads, and I would robotically go through the motions with a fake smile, holding back the visible irritation of knowing I was going to have to redo some of my work.

Then one day, I realized that I could scoop those salads in advance, seal up the bowls, and avoid the rework. All I had to do was keep those two small containers in the back corner of the display case and wait for Helen to arrive. You should have seen the smile on her face when she showed up and her quarter-pound of ham salad and coleslaw were ready to go.

After that, it became a personal challenge to find similar opportunities to decrease wasted labor or to anticipate shoppers' needs in order to impress. For example, the O'Brien family came in every Sunday morning after church, and each of them chose a doughnut from the case. The three kids were always disappointed if the sprinkled doughnuts were all gone. I realized that since I was in charge of dipping the doughnuts in sprinkles during my shift, I could help the children create their own doughnuts. One day, I asked each of the kids to tell me their names and their favorite colors. Two weeks later, during my next chance to wait on them, I surprised each O'Brien kid with a doughnut frosted in their favorite flavor and sprinkled with the preferred combination of colors. After I left that job in May 1982, I couldn't help but wonder what the kids said when someone else was wearing that smock on Sunday and the special doughnuts were gone.

Those salads and doughnuts didn't cost the store any extra, and providing them didn't take me any extra time. But the added "10¢" gesture of familiarity and anticipation of needs sure went a long way toward creating satisfied repeat customers.

Anticipate the Customer's Needs

The Power of Familiarity

As mentioned in the previous chapter, one of the most powerful customer-service skills that costs absolutely nothing is to create rapport through familiarity. Small gestures shown by staff can create loyal customers. And many of those gestures involve anticipating and even fulfilling needs before the customer even asks.

> **Small gestures shown by staff can create loyal customers.**

For example, we have a water cooler in our home, and I purchase several 5-gallon jugs of water at once and pick them up at the shop to avoid a delivery fee. Each time I go, there are several steps to the process, which, although simple, are a hassle.

I back the car up to the loading dock where the water is stored. Park the car, unload the empties, and carry the heavy refill jugs to the trunk. Then I drive around to the front of the store, park the car, get out and walk up a flight of stairs to see Rose, the team member behind the counter. I tell her my name, address, and how many jugs I took so she can add it to our monthly bill.

After about two years of doing this, one day I found myself loading the bottles during the early stages of a snowstorm. I glanced up to see Rose standing in the picture window behind her desk that faces the pick-up point. She held up three fingers to indicate that she needed confirmation that I had taken three bottles. I nodded yes and she gave me a thumbs-up and a wave. What she was saying through these non-verbal gestures was, "I recognize you, Laurie. I don't need you to come up those slippery stairs to tell me your address or how many bottles you took. Go ahead and leave and I will bill you. Have a nice day!" (Yes, all of that with just hand gestures.) It has been at least five years since this started, and I have not had a conversation beyond this special sign language since.

Simple story, simple action, but amazing impression. Rose remembers me and saves me hassle every time. There will be a time when I visit this business and someone else will be standing there. On that day, I will know how the O'Brien kids felt when the new girl didn't know to have their special doughnuts ready.

Anticipate the Customer's Needs

Sometimes familiarity isn't solving a guest's problem, it's simply making the encounter more pleasant. But isn't that what service is all about? Here's an example.

Not long ago, I was in line at the drive-through of my local Starbucks. They have the fancy video monitor that shows the barista a live picture of the driver. I had my window down waiting to order my venti vanilla latte when the car in front of me rolled into order position. I heard the barista speak first, saying, "Hello, Megan! Are you having your grande caramel macchiato today?" The driver of the Toyota replied happily, "I sure am Heather, thanks." When I got to the window, I got to meet Heather. She was full of genuine joy and happiness. I inquired as to how often she is able to memorize a frequent buyer's order like that. She smiled sheepishly and said, "Well, pretty often, actually."

I asked to take her picture and I posted the story to my Facebook page 10 minutes later, tagging Starbucks Corporate as well and gushing over her amazing customer service. Now, when I go through the drive-through during one of Heather's shifts, she remembers I am the one who took her picture and sung her praises. I have to admit, I'm disappointed when I hit one of her days off. What an asset she is to that organization. It's amazing how much more positive I feel after an encounter with her.

As these examples illustrate, making a connection doesn't have to be centered around a huge encounter. Sometimes it's the smallest "10¢" efforts that mean the most. Why can't everyone master this skill?

Anticipating someone's needs is a no-cost way to create a level of connection that matters.

Staying One Step Ahead

Later in life, when I worked for an ophthalmologist, he taught me that one way to differentiate myself as an assistant was to think one step ahead of the doctor. In other words, when I placed a patient in an exam room and I knew from my preparation that a certain test would be done, I should get that machine set up or obtain the particular instrument needed before the doctor appeared. All of these were huge time-savers for the doctor and, therefore, helped in our profitability. He once commented that his most valued surgical nurse in medical school was so good that "if she handed you something, you better figure out what to do with it." That statement always stuck with me and I worked hard to be one step in front of him all the time. How are you staying one step in front of your customers or your boss? Who doesn't appreciate having their needs met without even being asked?

I continue to be amazed at the number of times I experience a situation where the encounter could be better if swift action can be taken without hassle. Make time to talk to your supervisors about your level of empowerment and boundaries so you can stay one step ahead in your role.

Connecting Authentically

Sometimes you can't anticipate a customer's needs. And that's OK. If that's the case, intervene early in the encounter to find out how you can be of service. But when you do, be sure to be present and authentic. When you ask questions, turn on the active-listening button in your ears and your brain. When you don't, you actually can be creating a negative interaction. At the grocery store where I shop, employees have been trained to say the same thing every time you check out. "Did you find everything you were looking for?" At that point in the transaction, all of my groceries are up on the belt. Now is not the time for me to say that I couldn't find something. It would be more helpful if they asked that question when I'm in the aisle. But most often they just say "Hello" and "How are you?" when I am still shopping. That makes no sense to me. Those greetings should be reversed.

One day, I decided I would test the authenticity of the question. The person taking care of me was delightful. She smiled and greeted me in a friendly manner. She was doing everything right. Halfway through the transaction, she turned and said, "Did you find everything you were looking for?" I said, "Actually I need 8 ounces of Velveeta cheese, and I couldn't find it anywhere." I saw her shoulders slump a little bit. She replied in a slightly agitated voice "OK…" and turned on the call light to have another staff person find the cheese. Though she had the scripted line, she didn't have the authentic connection to match her reaction to my request.

Every guest is looking for an answer to something. Be the solution.

Every guest who seeks your company is looking for an answer to something. Be the solution. It can be as trivial as helping a customer find a particular product in a craft store or as serious as a visit to a dentist to find relief from excruciating pain. When a solution is provided—in any situation—a connection is made. Help your guests find the product or the service that delivers the answer to their needs, and they will be back. Authentic connections build rapport and must be a priority for your team.

But it's hard to be authentic or to be good at anticipating needs if you are too absorbed in your own behavior. Watch that you don't fall into the trap of a guest encounter being all about *you* instead of the guest. Once, I was at a resort that offered very expensive massages. I decided to treat myself and looked forward to the pampering. I went down to the spa and met my therapist. The moment the massage began, she told me about all the negative things in her life. She went on and on about a boyfriend, a demanding mother, even tales of a bad childhood. By the time the massage was over, all the negative energy had moved from her into me. Even though I was tenser than when the massage began, I was still expected to pay a lot of money for this experience. She didn't authentically connect with me. She made it all about her and nothing about me, which made it the worst massage I've ever had. I would never go back, and I would never recommend that spa.

Look for Simple, Creative Solutions

One unique concept for meeting a dining customers' needs is a "10¢" solution I wish would become an industry standard in the restaurant business. Give diners a small indicator card that signals to the server that either "we need something" or "we are fine just the way we are; leave us be." The Bubba Gump Shrimp Company is an example of how this works brilliantly. This restaurant, themed after the movie "Forrest Gump," uses every movie reference it possibly can. On each table is a ping-pong paddle with one side that says "Run, Forrest, Run" (a quote from the movie). When it's facing out, it signals the server to walk on by. The other side of the paddle is bright red and says "Stop, Forrest, Stop." Obviously, this side indicates we need something, and whichever server spots it first will stop and check in with us.

What I enjoy about this totally free service is that the response time is unbeatable when we need something. And when we are happily eating and talking, the staff doesn't interrupt great conversation. Have you ever been to a restaurant where the server is constantly interrupting to check on your satisfaction? Once we were at an establishment that was so attentive it became annoying. The server, the assistant manager, the manager, and the support staff clearing away dishes all asked us more than once how we were doing. I am sure they see it as great service, but we left there saying, "We're not going back anytime soon" because the constant interruptions created a disappointing experience.

I often travel alone with my work, and several times I have found myself in an awkward situation where I need to step away from my meal for one reason or another and I have no way of letting the dining team know not to take my plate. More than once, I have returned to my table to find everything gone except the dessert menu.

That's why I have created the personal plate card. It is meant for diners to put near their plate when they need to step away or to eliminate interruptions during an amazing conversation.

When I first came up with the idea to create one of these, I hesitated, thinking maybe I'm the only one who is aggravated when my needs are not anticipated correctly in this situation. I was sitting at an airport, writing this segment of the book, and I paused to contemplate whether it should stay or go. I couldn't believe it when I overhead a group of five businessmen discussing this exact topic. One of them said, "Yeah, I love their steaks, but the last time I was there I had to jump up to take a call and I had only taken a few bites. I came back and my whole damn plate was gone. They offered to cook me a new one, but I just said screw it. Really pissed me off." He was very animated in his retelling of the story, and his volume continued to rise as he finished the rest of the tale about his experience at this restaurant.

I had to resist the urge to interrupt the group and explain how freaked out I was that at that very moment I was trying to decide what to do about this segment of my book, and the answer came like a message from above. It was at that moment I decided to have the card designed so I could distribute it to as many people as possible. I hope it saves just one meal from being taken away prematurely or allows an engaged conversation to go on without constant interruptions.

Staying one step ahead of your customer will make a substantial difference. Acting on customer requests is just one element of delivering great service. By getting to know your guests, listening, and connecting with them, you'll be able to anticipate their needs before they even express them. That level of care and service is sure to keep them coming back for more.

Anticipate the Customer's Needs

Discussion Questions

In what areas of your business have you already succeeded in the power of familiarity?

What are the top 10 things your guests need or ask for on a regular basis?

Do you have systems in place to deliver frequently asked information before guests ask for it?

Are you empowered to identify needs and act on requests immediately?

What 10¢ decision is needed for your customers that is similar to the low-cost plate card?

Actions Speak Louder Than Words:
Going Beyond Verbal Communication

In most cases, actions speak louder than words. Your body communicates non-verbal messages. *Do you ever feel like your body language is misunderstood? Do you have "silent" habits that could be sending the wrong message?* It's important to understand the messages that you're sending before you even open your mouth. It's one of the ways you can generate the best first impression to help guests feel comfortable.

Building on My Body of Knowledge
After high school, I traded in my deli smock for a receptionist position at a chiropractor's office. This was my first introduction to healthcare, and I quickly found that I really enjoyed helping people feel better. After working there for six months, I made the choice to go to Palmer College of Chiropractic in Davenport, Iowa, to earn an assistant certificate. This education allowed me to take spinal X-rays and assist with certain treatments. After graduation, I started working with a practice closer to my new home in DeKalb, Illinois. During these formative years working for two different practices, I learned a great deal from the encounters I had with our patients and their families.

One unique aspect of this field of healthcare compared with most others is the frequency of patient visits. Because we saw patients on a regular basis for an extended period of time, it was easier to memorize their names, know what was important in their personal lives, and even create a professional relationship with the family members. I learned the importance of not only servicing our patients, but also tending to those who accompanied them in the door.

Actions Speak Louder Than Words

Even though I didn't own either of the practices where I worked during these years, that didn't stop my feeling of ownership in the business. I heard a consultant say, "The sign of a committed employee is one who behaves as if her name is on the side of the building, even when it isn't." That made an impression on me early in my career and likely influenced many of my choices.

The lesson that stands out so vividly in my memory about my first job in the healthcare field occurred when I was about 18. At that stage of my life, I hadn't yet learned about the impact of non-verbal communication. I had a habit of folding my arms over my midsection and leaning against the registration desk with a hip out and a little bit of attitude showing too. Those of you who have ever been the parents of teenagers know this pose. Of course, I thought I looked totally cool. Turns out I was the only one who thought so.

I was standing like that one day when the doctor I was working with walked up, pointed to my folded arms, and said, "Knock off the attitude!" I clearly remember responding, "What attitude?" with complete attitude all over my face. She handed me a book on body language and told me it was mandatory reading, complete with a book report.

I rolled my eyes and made a sound in my throat, both of which sent a crystal-clear statement that said, "This is stupid." She noted, "You will find those behaviors on page 52."

I took the book home against my will, and it's one of the five books that changed the course of my life. I had no idea that I was reeking of B.L. You've heard of someone reeking of B.O.? Same thing. Only the stinky messaging was my body language. Everything I was thinking was written all over my face all the time. What's scarier, sometimes what I *wasn't* thinking was written there too. Consequently, my face and I were easily misunderstood.

As soon as I learned how to change my body language, it made a difference in the rapport that I built, not only with the doctor, but with the patients as well. To this day, I share the importance of body language in almost every speech I give because of how important I believe it to be. And, while the change took time and a bit of self-education and self-awareness, it's a "10¢" change that has paid off handsomely throughout my career.

By the time I got to my second healthcare job when I was 22, I had the basics of body language down. I still had a lot to learn about the message my movements were sending, though. Being cognizant of the speed and purpose with which we move about in front of guests can send a silent signal as well. The clinical trainer at my job explained to me during my orientation that when you move in a highly efficient, but not hurried manner—walking quickly without running or performing tasks swiftly without appearing stressed— you give the message that you are on top of things. And she was right. Think about a time you have waited to be called back to an exam room in a clinic or waited for servers at a restaurant to notice you need something, yet they are hanging out, looking past you, or appearing as if they have nothing to do. This impacts your impression of the entire experience. Of course, it's possible someone else is in charge of your dining table, or maybe the room for your exam isn't available at the moment. However, because the staff is milling about without purposeful movement, you feel ignored.

The knowledge that my body—my facial expressions, posture, gestures, and even the intent of my movement—is speaking for me has stuck with me. That's why it's essential always to consider your actions just as thoughtfully as you do your words and to realize how much more influential you can be with improved body language.

Is My Body Language Showing?

It's important to consider the role of body language when it comes to making a first impression. Before you open your mouth to speak, you have already delivered a message. The words you speak, intertwined with your body language, communicate whether you are approachable or unapproachable, and so much more.

After studying my own body language, I learned how to change several key things. First, I adopted an open stance when engaging with people. That means arms not crossed, but rather down at my sides or loosely bent at the elbows with fingertips touching. Instead of leaning on things, which causes one hip to protrude and convey a cue of boredom, I trained myself to stand up straight with both feet firmly planted and my weight equally distributed.

Most important, I concentrated on making eye contact and smiling. Just like eye contact matters when talking to a customer, it makes a big impact with your internal customers and personal relationships as well. Maintaining eye contact doesn't mean staring at a person to the point of awkwardness. It means looking right at the person you are speaking to rather than over his/her shoulder or down at your feet. A smile doesn't have to be so big your cheeks hurt. A slight upturn of the corners of your mouth—just enough that it leaves the neutral position—is sufficient. Interestingly, a mouth in neutral position actually looks like attitude. A slight upturn makes all the difference.

Once I made these subtle changes, I noticed that my ability to connect with our guests and my co-workers improved. Now as a speaker meeting hundreds of new people each month, I am amazed at how strong the signal can be from those who have not studied the consequences of bad body language.

I recently gave a series of presentations to a group of healthcare providers at a community hospital. Some came with positive attitudes and body language that made me want to engage with them and learn more about their organization. Others came in with their posture and facial expressions silently screaming the opposite. Even though every person walking through that door was a stranger to me, my feelings toward them were not universal.

After one of the sessions, I commented to the executive monitoring the class that I had a few individuals with a lot of attitude in the session. He pointed to the section where a group of three had been sitting. "Was it the staff in the back right corner?" he asked. When I confirmed that it was, he said, "Yes, we have a lot of problems with that crew. In fact, it is *because of them* we are having this training." Wow, I can't imagine how embarrassed I would be if I found out an entire medical complex was having mandatory training because of *my* poor behavior.

Remember, not only should you think about the body language you "speak," you also need to learn how to read the body language of your customers. For example, in retail, closed-off body language—body turned away, avoiding eye contact, moving away when approached—tells you to back off and give the customer some space. Take notice of this and follow up with the right words, like, "Hey, let me give you some time to browse. Just wave at me if I can be of help." What about the opposite of that, when the customer's body language is signaling that they need our attention immediately—searching for assistance, a small hand wave and index finger raised slowly, or pacing while waiting are all silent indicators that a customer wants assistance.

Think about the body language of restaurant guests when they're in a rush. Picking up on that and leaving the check right after the plate is placed would meet their needs. Say something like, "I thought you might be in a hurry, so here's your check right away. I'll swing back in a little bit to see if you'd like anything else." Reading their silent signals will result in superior customer service, and a happy diner will likely be a repeat customer.

> To become a pro at body language, pay attention to the tells.

To become a pro at body language, pay attention to the tells. Small movements and gestures give you clues as to what a person thinks. Regardless of your business, apply the principles of non-verbal cues. It will be an impactful contributing factor to your overall success.

How to Handle the 'Overs'

When it comes to interpersonal interactions, one issue that is a cousin to body language is the ability to handle the "overs" you encounter. What in the world is an "over," and why do they need to be handled? Well, an "over" is a term I coined to describe a guest who is *over*-friendly, *over*-researched, or *over*bearing. They can make you uncomfortable, waste your time, or be downright threatening. What can you do to get out of each of these specific "over" situations?

Over-Friendly

Let's start with the over-friendly. Although it doesn't initially sound like a bad quality, many people feel uncomfortable with over-friendly guests in the workplace. I find it's especially true for young, attractive women who feel that patients or customers are crossing the line from friendly banter to pickup lines. However, it certainly is not limited to male offenders. Female guests can be just as guilty of crossing the line. To get out of an over-friendly situation, try this three-step approach:

1. Remove yourself from the encounter

Walk away to another part of the facility. Busy yourself with other work to create a physical distance between you and the over-friendly. When it is appropriate to reengage, be sure to stay professional and formal in your word choices.

2. Redirect the conversation

When dialogue first starts to sound over the line, redirect with statements like, "Bill, I can't allow you keep talking to me like that. I have to ask that we keep this conversation professional." Then immediately follow that up with an instruction related to the purpose of the encounter.

3. Refer to another team member

Discuss with your teammates the guest who makes you feel uncomfortable. If possible, refer the guest to another member of the team who can attend to his or her needs in your place. Being over-friendly can sometimes be rooted in insecurity. A person who is not feeling comfortable in a situation can change to a flirtatious approach in order to compensate. Knowing this helps me react appropriately toward this person.

Over-Researched

An example of an over-researched guest is a patient who presents in the exam room loaded with knowledge from the internet. She has a ream of paper that explains her self-diagnoses, the treatment plan, and a brand-new drug that will best work for her. She behaves as if all your office has to do is confirm and prescribe.

We all know that many times this data is going to be off-base or, at the very least, not the standard of care. The best thing you can do is protect the doctor's time by acknowledging the work that went into the research, showing appreciation for the participation in their care, and giving assurance that it will be shown to the doctor.

Here is a simple reply that meets all those criteria: "Jane, this is great research you've done, and we thank you for taking the time to bring it in today. Now, what I'm going to do is add this to your record, and I'll be sure Dr. Nelson knows that it's here. He's an expert when it comes to diabetes care. I can assure you that he is up to date on all the different options available to you."

By using the right words, you acknowledge the work that they put into their research without making any promises about how it will be implemented. Being proactive and gathering information gives the patient power at a time when they will need it.

This approach works in non-healthcare situations as well. Simply substitute the words applicable to your industry and you have the beginning of script that allows your team to handle the over-researched.

Overbearing

In the overbearing category, we find almost every other annoying characteristic that's difficult to handle. Over the years, I have dealt with people who have sworn at me, said cruel things, and even threatened the staff. In my personal life, I've dealt with overbearing people by avoiding them or getting away from them as fast as I can. In business, that isn't a choice. So, you have to know how to deal with them.

One thing that has really helped me is to try to see beyond the behavior that annoys me and remain unaffected by their words. Instead, I let it roll off my back and maybe even look for a chance to use humor. My favorite story about this was the time my patient was an older gentleman who was a priest. He seemed to have lost his verbal filter over the years, and he said anything that came to his mind. I was finishing up his testing when, out of the blue, he leaned out from behind the equipment and smirked, "You sure are fat."

Actions Speak Louder Than Words

Having been a plus-size gal most of my life, this was not news to me. But this overbearing older gentleman's rude remark caught me off-guard. I knew I couldn't be rude back to him. Instead, I went with humor. I stepped back, looked down at myself, and said incredulously, "What? I'm fat? You've got to be kidding me!" He burst out laughing, and I just went on with my work. My feelings were hurt, but I didn't show it.

One of my colleagues overheard what he said. She told the doctor we were working with what had happened. I found out later that when the doctor got into the room, he shook hands with the man and said, "I'm happy to take care of you today, sir, but I'm going to ask you to treat my team with the respect they deserve. Laurie works very hard for me, and I will not agree to take care of you as a new patient if you won't agree to be kind to the people I care about."

The man profusely apologized and asked to speak to me before leaving. He said he was very sorry and didn't know why he even said such a rude statement. Humor worked for me that day, but as you can tell, I'll never forget it. More than two decades later, when I needed to reflect on a person who was overbearing toward me, he was the person who first came to mind. Overbearing behavior comes from the fear of being incompetent. This gentleman was likely feeling vulnerable in the medical situation he was in, and he chose an overbearing attitude as a way to cope.

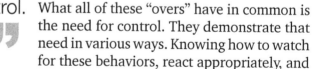

> What all of these "overs" have in common is the need for control.

What all of these "overs" have in common is the need for control. They demonstrate that need in various ways. Knowing how to watch for these behaviors, react appropriately, and remain professional is key. Combine that with a knowledge of how your silent signals play a role in your messaging and you will be a stronger communicator.

Taking Control of Conversations

As we learned with the overs, control isn't always about strength. It can manifest in many other ways, such as manipulation, intimidation, or the need to always be right.

If I said, "Let's play a game of tug-of-war," but gave you no other instructions, what would you do as soon as I handed your team the rope? Of course, you would pull as hard as you could against the other team and try to drag them to your side. That's because the object of tug-of-war is to get all players on the same side of the line using force. The team with more strength will pull the other side across the line for the win.

A lot of people make a mistake in business. We try to win others over by forcing them to see things our way. For example, a front-desk assistant says to a customer, "I'm sorry, but that's our policy. There isn't anything I can do about it." This is not a statement that will win over anybody. This scenario is like a tough game of tug-of-war. The customer pulls from one side of the desk, while the staff member pulls from the other. Both are determined to get their way.

But if you think creatively to solve challenges, you just might come up with a new way to provide a memorable guest experience.

Take another look at the instructions for tug-of-war and try replacing the word "force" with a different word and see how the situation changes. The object is to get all players on the same side of the line using *compromise*. "Well, we may be able to divide your fee into payments, but I'll need to ask you to put down at least a 50% deposit for us to offer that option."

Let's try another one. The object is to get all players on the same side with *bribery*. "We'd be able to knock a little off the fee if you let us put a sign in your yard that says we're the company doing your re-roofing work." You do something for us; we do something for you. Another common example of this tactic is when we say, "Today only. Buy one, get one free."

How about this one? Get everyone on the same side with *peer pressure*: "We're only five new members away from meeting our goal. What would it take to get you to sign up today as a new member?"

The list of examples could go on and on. Each one can work, but my favorite way to win someone to my side of the line is through *influence*. An influential statement might be, "I'm confident we can help you meet your goals with this new technology. Are you ready to learn how?"

Avoid making conversation into a tug-of-war. Look for ways to influence and find compromise. This will lead to amazing guest encounters.

If your customer-service levels aren't where you want them to be, start here. Work on improving your facial expressions, your non-verbal acknowledgments, and the quality of your personal interactions. Your attitude, body language, and word choice are all small changes in your behavior will lead to big wins in creating relationships and smoothing over conflicts.

Actions Speak Louder Than Words

Discussion Questions

How does the body language of team members create a feeling of approachability or unapproachability?

Does your body language always complement the words you are saying? If not, why not? If so, how do you know?

What specific areas of your body language need improvement?

Can you share examples of when co-workers or leadership had your back with a guest who was "over"?

Are there specific situations that occur with "overs" on a regular basis that need a plan for how to handle them smoothly?

Choosing Words Wisely:
Leveraging Language to Connect with Customers

Words, and how you say them, matter to your guests. Some words—both positive and negative—hold more weight than others. While it's bad form to use "50¢" words to make yourself sound smarter or more sophisticated, choosing words wisely is one of the most valuable 10¢ decisions you can make. The language you use can have a profound effect on how your service is perceived. *Do you choose your words wisely? How often do you find the right words elusive, causing you to say whatever pops into your head at the moment?* Use the techniques from this chapter to help you decide which messages help create positive encounters that will be remembered and shared.

The Art of Careful Communication
My in-depth training in customer service and scripting for superior communication began three years after I left the chiropractic field and began a new career in an ophthalmology practice in Sycamore, Illinois, called the Hauser-Ross Eye Institute. The co-founders, the husband-and-wife team of Drs. Lynn Hauser and Neil Ross, were light-years ahead of their time when it came to customer service in a healthcare setting. Not only were they amazing eye surgeons, they also had a talent for knowing how to make a patient feel special. When I joined their staff, I was only 22 years old and I had so much to learn.

It was clear to me from day one that the expectations of the staff were crystal clear. Over the years, many referring doctors asked me, "How did they find such amazing staff to join their team?" And the answer was, "They hired good people and then taught them how to behave." I don't know how to say it any clearer than that. We worked hard to put processes in place that helped us pick the very best person for an open position, but the magic was in providing clear behavioral expectations right out of the gate. If a person couldn't deliver service in the manner that matched our culture, then their time on board was short.

I believe if you ask any of the staff members who worked there over the years, they would tell you that treating our patients right was one of the most important things in our day. We were taught how to say things just right, without sounding robotic. We were expected to treat each other with respect and speak in a courteous way, especially in front of our guests. We made it our management mission to create the "Disney World of Eye Care," which is saying a lot. What does it take to make someone *want* to go to an eye surgeon? Once during a video shoot, I interviewed a gentleman about his experience with us in order to use it as a testimonial. Without any prompting from me, he said, "I wish I had a third eye so I could do it all again!" Now that is quite a compliment. But it didn't come without effort.

The lesson that stands out above all the rest during my time at Hauser-Ross came about eight months into my employment. We were growing very quickly, and I was offered a chance to advance from a receptionist role to a hands-on assistant. I escorted patients to exam rooms and learned how to perform preliminary testing prior to the doctor's exam. As an eager student, I was always looking for ways to do more and attempted to be the most helpful ophthalmic assistant possible. One day after prepping a particularly challenging patient, I made the mistake of thinking it would be a good idea to warn Dr. Ross what he would face when he entered the room. I took a small yellow sticky note and wrote "FYI, this patient is a little snotty" and stuck it to the outside of her chart before placing it in the holder outside the door.

I laugh about it now, because why did I think needed to warn Dr. Ross about the patient when he was quite capable of handling any situation? Why did I choose those immature words? Didn't it occur to me that the patient might see the note at some point in the visit? Well, lucky for me, she never saw it. From down the hall I watched the doctor read it, pull it off the chart before entering the room, and slide it carefully into his lab-coat pocket.

The "teachable moment" came at the end of the day. That's code for "learn what you did wrong and promise to do better next time." All these years later, I can remember what he said to me almost word for word: "Laurie, I really appreciate you trying to warn me in advance what mood the patient was in. That is very helpful." Since he started with a compliment, I was already standing up a little straighter and silently congratulating myself on what a fantastic help I was to him. That emotion was very short-lived, though, because of what came next. He continued, "However, it is very possible that the patient could have seen the note and, with the words you chose, it might have been offensive to her." True. Calling someone snotty isn't going to make them feel very wanted. "In the future, when you need to alert me to a situation where a person is angry or, as you say, 'snotty,' let's use the word *concerned* instead. Around here, let's make that our universal word for 'unhappy,' OK?" Embarrassed, I excused myself from his office and I *never* made that mistake again. I immediately started choosing words carefully, and overnight I saw the impact words could have in almost any situation. I had no idea that wordsmithing would become one of my superpowers.

Eighteen years later, when I resigned my position to start my professional speaking career, I was given a chance to see my personnel file for the first time. I turned the pages one by one, going backward in time through annual evaluation pages, copies of certificates of achievement, and random notes about a variety of things related to my long employment. But at the very bottom of the file, taped to a piece of typing paper, was that sticky note. Next to it in Dr. Ross' instantly identifiable handwriting was the date that it happened and the simple notation: "Spoke with Laurie about this, she seemed to understand."

Scripting for Superior Communication

Scripting for superior communication means using the right word at the right time for a desired result. Avoid the robotic: "Do you want fries with that?" Instead, put words together in a professional, thoughtful way that communicates great service.

An often-overlooked technique in customer service, scripting can make a big difference in the impression you give your guests. It involves small, simple changes in word choice that create a big difference in perceived service levels. For example, a customer at a retail location asks where a certain item is located. The response could be, "It's over there in aisle three." The better, scripted response is, "I'd be happy to show you. Please follow me." The difference is that we feel totally engaged with the person who used the more service-oriented scripted response.

> Scripting means using the right word at the right time for a desired result.

Just because you're following a script doesn't mean that you stop being present in the conversation or sound so orchestrated that you are a word-for-word responder like an audio recording that says the same thing every time. Scripting simply means finding words and phrases as sentence starters that connect and engage with the person you are communicating with, rather than choosing words that agitate or are disengaging.

Although I give credit to learning scripting at my job in eye care, I was actually exposed to the concept at a much earlier age when my father taught me the "IBHT Attitude." My dad would come in from a night of farming, go upstairs to take a shower, and then settle into his La-Z-Boy in the living room. On more than one occasion, he would turn to me and ask, "Pumpkin, will you run upstairs and get my slippers?" Boy, did this drive me crazy. Dad was just upstairs, why couldn't he remember to get the slippers himself? One day I decided to educate my father to that fact. I said, "Dad, you were just upstairs. Why didn't you get your slippers yourself?" He then proceeded to teach me the best four words I've ever learned in my life. He explained, "Laurie, I'm your dad, and when I ask you to do something, you would be much better off saying 'I'd be happy to.' I will feel better about asking you, and you will feel better about doing it." I didn't understand at the time; I just went and got his slippers without fuss. But the IBHT lesson remained with me. Years later, when I started working at the eye clinic and was taught the concept of scripting, I recognized the technique as a "slipper moment" and changed words in my sentences to communicate better.

Just like the words I'd be happy to send a favorable message, listen to the difference between these scripts.

Version 1: *It's going to cost you about $259 for this.*
Version 2: *The fee for that service is $259.*

Version 1: *Unfortunately, he's not here right now.*
Version 2: *Mike's not available at the moment. May I leave him a message, or is there something I can help you with?*

Version 1: *If you want to wait over there, the manager will be with you in a minute.*
Version 2: *If you'll please make yourself comfortable in this area, we'll escort you to the conference room as soon as possible.*

Though the end result is no different between version 1 and version 2, the way we feel about the customer service differs vastly.

Taboo Words and Phrases

Another area that falls under the topic of scripting is my taboo-word list. These are words that your team should avoid using. Of course, the list varies among industries. Here I've chosen my top five universal taboo words and provided replacement words or phrases.

1. No

The first taboo word is "no." Replace it with the word "*actually.*" When somebody asks, "Can I expect to receive that order tomorrow?" and you reply, "No, it's not going to be here," it comes across as rude. If you respond instead, "Actually, it's due to arrive on Friday," it sounds courteous. When a restaurant patron asks for salad as a substitution but that isn't allowed, a server might be heard saying, "No, we don't allow any substitutions." Instead, consider saying, "Actually, the meals are served as listed, but I can add a side salad for just $1.99 more. Would you like that?"

2. Busy

Another taboo word at one office where I worked was the word "*busy.*" Our manager thought this word felt too blunt, and she was right. Listen to how this sentence sounds: "No, I can't put your call through to Mike; he's busy right now." That makes the customer feel pretty low-priority, doesn't it? Compare that with this revised statement: "Actually, Mike is currently assisting other customers. May I put you through to his voicemail so he can get back to you as soon as possible?" There's a huge difference in how the words feel to the listener.

3. There's nothing we/I can do

Next is the expression "*There's nothing we/I can do.*" That's like throwing gasoline on a fire. There is *always* something more you can do. You can listen, empathize, or redirect. An equally irritating partner to this statement is "*That's our policy.*"

In both cases, being able to redirect a person or explain the situation with more palatable words can make all the difference. For example, a teacher might say, "The grade has already posted and there is nothing more I can do." Or he could say, "Actually, your son earned a D- on the test; however, there's an extra-credit opportunity coming up next week. I suggest he do that to try to raise his semester grade." The responsibility is shifted from teacher to student, where it rightfully belongs.

Another example of this issue is a park district that had installed new playground equipment that included a small rock-climbing wall. In the first week, several children fell off the wall and received minor scrapes. The board decided to have the staff place a sign on the wall that said, "No Climbing." When parents started to complain, the staff got into the habit of saying, "I'm sorry, that's our policy." This doesn't really help when a parent is confused about why an apparatus designed for play isn't allowed to be used. I coached them to change the sentence to, "We have found that a few children have been slightly injured from crawling too high, so we are encouraging kids to play with the other new pieces of equipment until we are able to install the foam mat below." We can accept the rules better if we understand why they exist.

4. Honey/Sweetie/Toots or any other term of endearment that is not earned

Adding on a quick little endearment at the end of a sentence with customers has its proper place and time for use. Where it doesn't work is when no relationship has been established and the service provided uses the over-the-top familiar tone to go with it. Examples like, "What can I get for you today, hon?" or "Sweetie, you just let me know if you need anything" are agitating to most customers. Training oneself to stop saying them when it is habit can be hard, but the difference is very noticeable.

5. Sorry

The final suggested word swap is, in my opinion, one of the most valuable to learn. Stop making unnecessary "sorry" statements. Many companies are quick to say "I'm sorry" because they believe the statement comes across as great service. That's not true. For example, a travel advisor hears from a client upon return from their trip that it did not meet their expectations, and the advisor says, "I'm so sorry you had a bad trip." If it isn't the fault of the advisor, then I suggest changing that sentence to: "I'm certainly disappointed to hear that. Tell me what happened." This simple change shows empathy without absorbing unnecessary blame.

...save your "sorries" for when an apology is owed.

I urge you to save your "sorries" for when an apology is owed. I'm amazed at how often I see "sorry" signs that could be worded differently. Several years ago, I was in an electronics store with a choice of four cash registers to ring up purchases. Two of them were open with no waiting. The fourth lane had a sign on it that read, "Sorry for the inconvenience. This register temporarily closed." First, I noticed the sign was a professionally printed one, so there was nothing temporary about the situation. If it had been printed on a piece of typing paper with marker, I might have believed them. But it wasn't. This sign was used daily and put in front of any register they didn't want to use as a way of saying, "Nope, not using this lane."

"Sorry" is the first word on the sign. Way back in their subconscious minds when customers see "sorry," they may feel slighted rather than served. The sign should read, "We would be delighted to help you at any one of our open registers." See how much better that sounds?

The formula is quite simple: Creativity + Humor = Connection.

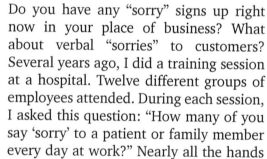

Do you have any "sorry" signs up right now in your place of business? What about verbal "sorries" to customers? Several years ago, I did a training session at a hospital. Twelve different groups of employees attended. During each session, I asked this question: "How many of you say 'sorry' to a patient or family member every day at work?" Nearly all the hands went up in every class. That means that this organization says "sorry" more than 9,125 times per year to their patients and patients' families. Great service? No.

The hospital was in the middle of a remodel. The sign in the lobby and the message on the radio ad they ran said, "Sorry for the mess." I encouraged them to change the ad to say, "Guess what? We're renovating to help serve you better." Since that session, I've asked many audiences the same question, "Do you say 'sorry' to at least one customer every day?" Because the response has been an overwhelming "yes," it made me realize what a big deal this is.

Choosing Words Wisely

We build rapport by making a connection with our words. When appropriate, adding a little creativity and some humor can also build a connection. The formula is quite simple: Creativity + Humor = Connection.

For example, the management team at Kampgrounds of America (KOA) took action on this idea immediately after our training session. I've learned that those in the tourism industry use a lot of sorry statements. It's the nature of the beast, I guess. Throughout their locations, they were using several "sorry" signs. But by doing slight "10¢" wordsmithing and adding a dash of humor, those apologies can create a new emotional reaction. Here are the replacement signs they implemented immediately:

Broken-toilet sign: *Plungers Needed: Interested parties apply within.*

Change machine that is out of money: *Selfish Change Machine. Machine is not in the giving mood. Currently only taking money.*

Out-of-order washing machine: *Don't Pick This One! Machine not living up to its full potential. Please use another.*

See how using slight humor is better than the sorry word?

While grocery shopping, I spotted a Planters® peanut display with a pad of coupons attached to it. Consumers were supposed to rip off the top coupon for $2 off their purchase. When all the coupons were gone, the remaining card read in large capital letters, "*Sorry! All coupons have been depleted.*" What made the message even worse was that there were five of the empty displays lined up next to each other. So, when I came around the corner pushing my shopping cart, *all I saw was Sorry! Sorry! Sorry!* all over the place. I wrote a letter to Planters explaining all about word swapping for better connecting. I encouraged them to use humor and change the display to read "*Nuts! Your neighbor beat you to it!*" I've never heard back from Planters (not even a case of cashews as a "thanks for the idea" gift).

What about the use of "sorry" in your email correspondence or your outbound voicemail message? After two days away at a continuing-education event, do you reply to your stacked-up emails by saying,

"I'm so sorry I didn't respond sooner to your email"? Instead, you could say, "It's Monday and I am happy to be back in the office after an educational symposium. I'm ready to provide you an answer to your question." The word choice in the second example conveys a totally different emotion. It implies that your absence actually served your customers well, rather than inconveniencing them.

Does your standard outbound voicemail say, "Hi, this is Jackie Larson of JL Realty. I'm sorry I'm not here to take your call right now. Please leave your name, number, and the time of your call and I will get back to you as soon as possible"? You have just missed a chance for a 15-second commercial. How much better would it be if instead it said, "Hi, this is Jackie Larson, and I'm out helping people just like you find the perfect house to buy. Please let me know that you have called, and we will get started helping you next!" Beep.

There are two times when I believe a sorry statement is highly appropriate and should be used. First, when an apology is owed to the guest. If we have made a mistake or there is an oversight, we need to validate the concerns with regret. The second time it is good to use sorry is when you want to express a true sign of empathy. "I'm sorry you are going through this." Or "I'm sorry to hear about your loss" are both excellent examples of the proper use of the word. The sorries I am suggesting that you remove are the unnecessary, habitual ones. Once you've raise your awareness of the sorry statement, you will realize how prolific it is in service industries. Take a tour of your building and look for the "sorry" signs. Revise what you say to convey the information without the apology. Discuss how often and in what situation you find yourself apologizing to your guests. When you determine that an apology is owed, find the best way to say it. If you decide an apology isn't owed or it's just a habit, start creating your list of replacement sentences.

Be Specific in Your Word Choice

A colleague of mine from my eye-care days recently shared with me that her biggest lesson about word selection is one that has stuck with her for the rest of her career. As a medical scribe, she went with the doctor to every room and completed all the charting in real time.

Choosing Words Wisely

When it was time to escort a patient to the next step of the process, she was responsible for communicating what to expect. One day, she said to a patient, "If you would like to stay right here, someone will be in to get you shortly to perform that test." Overhearing what she said, the doctor pulled her aside to quietly provide her with a "teachable moment." He said, "When you use the word 'someone,' it's not specific enough. It sounds like anyone off the street could just come in and do the task. I want you to say a 'technician' will be here shortly to perform that test." By simply replacing that one word, more credibility is given to the position and the communication is much more professional.

Along the same lines, for those of you who are in healthcare, remember not to call patients by what they need, such as, "Hey, we got a Pap in room two." There's not a Pap in room two. Theresa Lansing is in room two. Instead, use a phrase like: "There's a patient who needs a Pap test in room two." Small change in word choice, big change in how it's perceived if it's overheard.

I remember reading an article years ago about a man visiting a café and ordering the blue-plate special, which was a pork chop. It came with a choice of potato or vegetable, but the server forgot to ask him which side he wanted. He started to read his paper as she walked away. Then she turned and yelled, "Hey, pork chop!" He, of course, didn't realize she was talking to him, so he glanced over his shoulder to see just who this pork chop guy was. When he turned back around, she pointed to him and said, "Yeah, you, pork chop... potato or green beans?" She was calling him "pork chop" because that's what he had ordered. His point in the article was that we should call a person by name or at least come back and refer to him as "sir" or get his attention in some way. Calling him "pork chop" certainly isn't the path to excellent customer service.

Remember, if scripting isn't used, you and your co-workers will bring your own personalities and previous experiences in communication to the position. If you naturally excel at this skill, you're all set. But years of training have taught me that many need help with this concept.

Use Words to Reframe Your Position

Reframing issues, a specialized topic in communication, helps restructure thinking and address problems. Because mindsets are powerful and influence future choices, behaviors, and word selection, successful reframing puts your organization in a favorable position through accurate communication. When should you consider reframing your issues? When the public perception of a situation is skewed or when false information is floating in your marketplace, consider reframing.

Domino's Pizza provides a well-known example of reframing. For years, they had a reputation for subpar pizza. A few years back they tackled the issue head-on in their advertising, which said: "We want to make our pizza taste better." They called it as people saw it, which was a very bold move. It was also a great way to reframe how consumers felt about the product. Most of the time, thinking in advance about framing the issue pays off. If there's a false rumor surrounding your organization, especially if there may be truth to the gossip, you need to take a stand for your position.

Rumor has it the other fun thing they started at Domino's is taking "special requests" when you order your pizza. My teenage daughter, who is an aspiring artist, was the first to alert me to this new craze. She talked me into adding to the digital order form: "Draw a picture of a dog and give him a cute name." When the pizza arrived, she raced to the door to find out if it actually worked. There on the inside of the lid was one of the worst stick-dog drawings ever, complete with a dog tag that said "cute name." Since that time, I have done a little online research on this concept and, sure enough, there are hundreds of examples of funny requests carried out by Domino's employees. What a great way to reframe their reputation.

To reframe an issue and avoid pitfalls, begin by asking these questions:
- What is the issue?
- Who's involved?
- What led to the problem?
- What's the best solution?
- Does the public need to know about this?
- How will public opinion be different after we reframe?

Choosing Words Wisely

While this may seem like a management and business-owner problem, frontline staff can play a large role in keeping these issues from evolving. Sharing inside gossip at neighborhood parties with friends and family exacerbates the rumor mill. Like the old game of telephone, the retelling of data is rarely exactly the same. By the time it has passed between several people, the message becomes unrecognizable from the original.

Though this is certainly easier said than done, remember that what goes on at work should stay at work. Before you open your mouth, consider the image your words might send to the community. If a friend asks, "How are things going at work?" and you respond, "Man, I'm telling you, things are so messed up over there. I don't know how much longer we can even keep the doors open," you just pushed yourself one more millimeter closer to being out of a job. Instead, reframe the issue in positive language. Say something like, "Well, things have been stressful lately, but I really believe in the work we're doing. I'm hoping the new management will make things easier."

When you reframe your image, remember to choose words to your advantage. As a team, discuss whether you need to reframe current issues in the marketplace. If you do, then develop a deliberate campaign to improve your image.

The best example I have ever seen of reframing an issue was at the America's Brewpub in Aurora, Illinois. Walter Payton, the famous Chicago Bears running back, was a co-owner in the establishment, which was a local favorite hangout. In 1999, when word of his terminal cancer spread through the region, the rumor started that the restaurant was closing down. Because we really liked the place, we hurried up and made a trip there just in case it was true. On each table was a sign in an acrylic, self-standing frame that hit every component of a reframing campaign. I was so taken by how well done it was, I asked our server if I could have a copy of it for my

Choosing Words Wisely

files. I knew one day I would include it in a book on the power of words. It read:

> *Why Walter? Is the question asked by most people. We don't really think people expect an answer. But we at America's Brewpub think we have one.*
>
> *There is a tremendous shortage of "donor organs" available in this country. Attempts to raise the public awareness of the need have always fallen short.*
>
> *Walter's illness has raised public awareness to an all-time high. We are convinced that by the time Walter gets his transplant and fully recovers from this ordeal, the donor registration throughout the country will be at the most efficient level in history. And that because of this availability...waiting times will be considerably reduced.*
>
> *We do not know of any other person who could accomplish so much in such a short period of time.*
>
> *Sign your donor card (back of your Driver's License) here at the Roundhouse and have a manager sign as your witness and we will give you a $10 gift certificate.*
>
> *Just tell your server you would like to have a manager witness your donor card and we'll take care of the rest.*
>
> *Thanks for your support, America's Brewpub*

We signed the back of our license that night. Not for the $10 gift card, but as a small sign of support for the cause. Walter passed away in early November of that year, but the restaurant continued on for several more years. Today it is owned by a different group of people, but the point is, the doors are still open.

What did this reframing accomplish? Several things. First, it showed that no one ever gave up hope on Walter. Second, because the restaurant gave us a coupon and invited us to return, it sent the message that it wasn't closing its doors anytime soon. This simple

Choosing Words Wisely

"10¢" note to reframe our thinking put the only possible positive spin on a horrible situation—and hopefully encouraged others to become registered organ donors like we did. It was a valuable lesson that words matter.

Tone That Connects

Not only do words matter, but the tone that we use when saying them certainly makes a difference too. We all have heard the old adage *It's not always what you say, but how you say it!*

At the chiropractic clinic where I worked, I had a colleague named Donna who excelled at her responsive communication. She had a warm tone to her voice and a genuineness to her personality that set her apart from the rest of us. As a lifelong local, she knew many of the patients and had connections to them. I noticed that when we had to converse with a patient about something sensitive, like an unpaid bill, she had an ease about her and changed her way of communicating. In my training, I refer to this as using "the backyard tone." Instead of being formal or strict about policies and using words like, "Mr. Jones, we show you have $257 due on your account, and I will need you to pay that today before your care begins," Donna would say it like this: "Hank, it looks like I have to ask you for about 257 bucks today. Can we make that work?"

Can you hear the difference those small changes make? The second one sounds like something you would say to a friend at a backyard barbecue, and it works! Nobody ever said no to Donna.

Today, I use that tone in many of my own business dealings. Just the other day, a complete stranger called to talk to me about something that could have been awkward. But instead, I did "The Donna." I used a tone of familiarity and chose words that kept the dialogue very light and conversational, like we were old friends just chatting at a party. It made such a difference to the flow of the call, and the result was a positive one.

Choosing Words Wisely

The impact of our word choices cannot be underestimated. If you don't have a training program available to help you in choosing the right words for your position, I encourage you to reach out and ask for guidance from either a mentor inside the business or from a supervisor. If you are reading this and know that you already excel at verbal skills, consider being a mentor to others who may not be as fortunate.

When the lessons on body language are combined with influential word choices, your service levels will be unbeatable.

Choosing Words Wisely

Discussion Questions

What key phrases are in need of a word replacement for better results at your organization?

Are you allowed to change words and phrases as you see fit, or do you need management approval?

As an individual, are there certain words you use with frequency that should be taboo?

Is your team guilty of calling customers by what they need instead of by their name?

Are there issues that need reframing in your company? Or, if you are an individual reading this book, do you have personal-mindset issues that need reframing in order for you to grow in your position or be happier in life?

Secrets of an Undercover Shopper:
Seeing Our Service from a Different Perspective

Often, we wear down in our customer-service performance not because we don't know how to do it, but because we have grown tired. *Has service fatigue impacted your execution of duties? What would you say if you found out your last customer was a secret shopper?* By reviewing our work performance through the eyes of our customer, we can spot areas for improvement.

Game Invention with a Mystery Twist

Even though my healthcare career allowed me to earn a nice living working for someone else, I never lost the desire to be an entrepreneur. The possibility of making something up, developing it into an idea that people will pay for, and then finding a way to sell the product has always been thrilling for me. I don't anticipate that feeling will ever end.

An opportunity to use a very different creative muscle came when an old friend of mine was planning to host a murder-mystery party at his home. However, the prepackaged games on the market were designed for only six to eight players, and, on top of that, the games appeared to be rather lame. He and his wife wanted to host an innovative party for 12 people and asked if I would be interested in creating a unique game. I jumped at the chance, and the party was a blast. Within a short time, my husband, Tom, and I put together an extremely creative murder-mystery party side business, which we ran for several years. We had two games. One was our original creation, a birthday dinner party for 12. The other was a class-reunion theme that could accommodate up to 100 people at corporate events. McDonald's was our first client for the big party. It was a social outing for the franchise division, and they anticipated about 90 people. The pressure was on for the new game inventors.

Tom and I created a character for each guest, and the character profiles were delivered to them in advance so they could dress and act the part. It was so much fun to watch people arrive who were complete strangers to us, yet we knew which character they were playing by how closely they matched our descriptions. Our favorite character, and the most easily identified, was a guy named Bobby Jo Zaleski, a blind country singer who was famous for his hit song called "Bein' Blind Ain't Bad If You've Seen the Women I've Dated."

Watching a multitude of grown-ups pretending to be people they are not was very exciting. It must be how a screenplay writer feels when he sees the end result of his imaginary people appearing on the screen in the theater. Most people were so good at bluffing, I realized I could take this creative idea to market and put a twist on the mystery-shopping industry. One of my star murder-mystery attendees was the first person I approached to give this crazy plan a try in the real world. And what a journey we've had.

Making Money for Pretending

When I was in the very early stages of a speaking career, it wasn't too difficult for me to secure work in my niche industry of eye care. But as I became interested in branching out to other businesses in my area, I knew I needed to add a twist to the customer-service basics. The "aha" moment for secret shopping came in 2001, when our chamber of commerce joined with our sister city to provide a joint educational day on customer service for small-business owners and managers. An impressive number of people showed interest for a small-town event, with 57 companies committed to attend. As I looked over the registration list about two weeks before the meeting, I had a moment of self-doubt. I personally knew more than half of the people coming. It is an undisputed fact that speaking in front of peers, friends, and colleagues is much harder than speaking to a room of strangers. Confidence in my content wasn't the issue. I was more concerned that they would brush off the customer-service ideas as too basic for the level of owner, CEO, and top-tier management personnel who were coming.

One particular company on the list—which shall remain nameless in case the owner ever reads this book—is known for poor service in my community. I saw the name of the person who would represent them that day, and I knew for a fact that he believed his company was superior in their service levels. How does one tell him he's wrong? Certainly, I can't do that in front of a room of his peers; more important, what evidence do I have that they fall short in service? What if I could prove to myself that word on the street was right? No doubt that would that give me a stronger leg to stand on when it was showtime.

Then it hit me. I could ask one of my friends from the murder-mystery party to go into his place of business and pretend to be a customer. Instantly, I was excited about the idea. I created a very short list of criteria for her and trained her on what I wanted evaluated and tips on how I thought she could conduct herself to accurately play the role of a new customer in this particular industry. It worked perfectly! The company did an average job of meeting her customer-service expectations. It wasn't horrible, but she was still able to give me excellent suggestions for how they could have done better.

Then I thought to myself, "What would happen if I personally shopped all the pre-registered companies?" With only 12 days left until the program, it would be a challenge. While the time investment was high, it was otherwise a free endeavor. It was a 10¢ decision that I was pretty sure would pay off. So, I got busy.

Step one was to create a customer-service audit report. It started out with 10 simple things I expect to receive when being taken care of as a customer. Over time, it has expanded to the 32-point audit that exists today. I decided that the rating scale should be very simple: Excellent, Good, Average, Needs Improvement. Then I spent four full days trying to do business as a "new guest" with every one of the attendees.

What I found was fascinating. First, it was very easy to pick out the top three high-performing organizations based on their total scores. Equally uncomplicated was the task of choosing three honorable mentions for an *individual* within an organization who did one specific noteworthy act. But the overall experience did not place the company in medal position. That's right, I gave out gold, silver, and bronze awards with corresponding prizes as part of my content. It made sense to me to recognize the winners with public praise and to give the rest of the attendees their confidential report in a sealed envelope.

When the big day arrived, I was giddy with anticipation of how my investigative study would be perceived. I was the only one who knew I had done this task, so the reveal was sure to be a twist to the normal meetings they experienced. After my introduction, I started with 101-level material. Since I was talking to the highest-level executives, I anticipated that their looks would be of slight boredom and possibly impatience that the material was too simple.

As planned, after about 10 minutes, I stopped abruptly mid-sentence and said, "I'm going to stop for a moment."

There was a long pause, and all eyes shifted up to meet my gaze.

I continued, "I'm getting the impression that this content is too basic for you; is that right?" Several heads nodded, clearly signaling agreement for the entire crowd.

Then, I delivered the twist. "Well, that's good to hear, because I've tried to do business with all of your companies within the past two weeks, and I'm going to spend the remaining time of my presentation telling you who in this room totally rocked it, and who fell a little short." I took a long pause to let that sink in, with an "uh-oh" look on my face that conveyed the message that trouble might be coming for a few of them.

Secrets of an Undercover Shopper

A man in the front row muttered under his breath, but loud enough for others to hear, "Oh, crap." Everyone in the room laughed because they were thinking the exact same thing. In fact, almost every single time I have done this form of reveal in the two decades since, I get the exact same reaction with varying degrees of vulgarity on the word "crap."

I continued, "I think customer service and weight loss have a lot in common. I've battled a weight problem my entire life. A few years ago, I went to see the doctor. He said, 'Laurie, I've got to ask you a question. How is it possible that a motivational speaker can have a weight problem?' I said, 'Well, that's easy. I see the golden arches, I'm motivated to turn in.'"

...knowing and doing are two very different things.

We all know that if you burn more than you eat, you'll lose weight. But knowing and *doing* are two very different things. I believe customer service works the same way. We can teach the basics of customer service, but is the staff really doing it? These business owners were about to find out.

For the next 50 minutes, I told tales of my secret shopping in our two neighboring communities, making sure to keep it light and positive, yet impactful. No one was doodling, nor did a single person leave their seat to use the washroom. They waited with bated breath to find out if their teams had performed at a level that was praiseworthy.

I truly feel it was some of the best work I have ever done, and a secret-shopping division of my company was born that day. Since then, we have shopped hundreds of businesses by phone and in person. Our approach to this task is a little different than what is done by the bigger companies that offer this service. Many will look for behaviors that match brand standards, like a convenience store that is tested on compliance with checking IDs before selling tobacco, or a bank teller who uses the exact right phrases to upsell banking products. Our approach is extremely subjective. Our shoppers are given the criteria to judge on our scale, but then they provide a rating strictly based on their own opinion. I want the report to be exactly the response a real customer would have after an encounter with the company. It's probable that two different people will experience the exact same situation with different reactions and ratings.

For example, a bank hired me to evaluate them with multiple shoppers. I sent two women into a small branch on a "casual Friday" in July. Shopper #1 was a recent college graduate. Shopper #2 was a businesswoman in her late 50s. The bank employee was dressed in a very short denim skirt and adorable flip-flops, and she presented with a bubbly personality. At least that's how shopper #1 described her after giving "Brittney" the highest ratings possible in all categories. Shopper #2 came from a corporate background where a professional wears a knee-length skirt, nylons, and sensible pumps for a day at work. She was so put off by the appearance of "Banker Brittney" that she had to call me from the road to share her amazement that the company would allow employees to dress like this. She found her demeanor way too casual and inappropriate, and, as a result, rated her below average in most categories. Same day, same staff person, two very different reports.

In my presentation to the branch managers later that month, I shared this anecdote. We discussed the fact that generations see these situations differently and we must have policies that reflect that. Should there be a stricter dress code, or would it be better to create a fresh, hip vibe for the bank? In the end, they decided that a majority of their walk-in bank clientele fit the demographic of my second shopper, the more conservative of the two. In this case, I would agree, but I've been in other scenarios where changing up the old way of doing things is the better choice. Point being, there is no one right answer. As most of my favorite lawyers always say, "It depends."

One of my big regrets is that I didn't start a detailed journal of the secret-shopping experiences we have had over the past two decades. It would have made a great book in its own right! But the good news is my memory is strong. Following are the top keeper moments that may interest you, along with the takeaway lessons.

Secret-Shopping Fails

Third-place finisher: Failure to use the provided training script

A doctor asked me to do a secret-shopping phone call to his office. He wanted me to pretend to be a new patient. His hope was that the staff person answering the phone would give me an explanation of his great attributes, including where he'd graduated from medical school and the several industry awards he had received. These are things that he thought were important to a new patient.

I asked him, "How confident are you that when I call, your receptionist is going to do the spiel just the way you scripted it?" He said, "I am extremely confident. We've gone over it. She knows how to do it. She's practiced it. All is good." Satisfied with his response, I called the next day. During the entire phone conversation, the receptionist did a fantastic job of taking care of my needs. However, as we neared the end of the phone call, she hadn't yet fulfilled the job of presenting her doctor in the positive light that he expected. Because I wanted her to score well on this test, I asked a leading question in hopes it would cause her to recite some of the scripted words from her training. I said, "You know, before I let you go, I'm kind of new to the area. Is there something you could tell me about your doctor to reassure me he's the best choice for me?" Now, what more could I have done for her? I gave her a perfect opportunity to use the scripted line. After a long pause, she said, "Well, he's 6 foot, blonde, and gorgeous. What more do you need to know?"

> ...even though we train the script, it doesn't mean the staff is sticking to it consistently.

When the report went back to the doctor, although flattered, he was disappointed. His employee hadn't performed as he expected—or how she'd been trained. The experience made him realize that even though we train the script, it doesn't mean the staff is sticking to it consistently.

Second-place finisher: Unable to make a sale due to behavior choice

One of my most memorable undercover experiences took place at a dry cleaner. I entered the shop with the storyline of a bride, 20 years past her wedding day, who still had her gown rolled up in a bag. I stated that I had been procrastinating about having it preserved and I was there to inquire about the process and how much it would cost. The person helping me was a young man with "assistant manager" written on his nametag. After I stated my reason for being there, he reached behind him, grabbed a flyer with a picture of a wedding dress, a few bullet points, and a starburst in the upper-right corner that said $99. Without saying a single syllable, he plopped it in front of me and pointed to the cost. I gave him an opportunity to accompany this gesture with some words, but none came. After many seconds of awkward silence, I finally said, "Oh wow, that was more than I thought it would be." (Let's see what he does with price objection.) With a dismissive wave over his shoulder he replied, "Well, there's a place in (insert name of next town over) that will do it for $69."

A few weeks later, at the event where the owner of the dry cleaner attended my reveal, we distributed the confidential reports. She approached me privately after reading it to ask how confident I was that my shopper had recorded this experience accurately. I had to share that I personally was the shopper for this visit and that the words alone did not do justice to the experience. I then reenacted the entire scenario, imitating the body language that can't properly be described in words. She was horrified but the experience taught her an important lesson. If the staff do not feel comfortable quoting prices or do not fully understand the fees, it will be reflected in their communication. We see this *very often* when we shop.

Secrets of an Undercover Shopper

First-place finisher: Missed opportunity due to process gap

The secret-shopping story that I consider the biggest fail occurred when a banking system hired us to shop 17 locations to see how well the staff would greet a potential new customer who was looking to open any kind of account.

I entered each bank with the same storyline. "Hi, I'm new to the area and I wanted to learn more about the different accounts you have available here that will fit my needs." Imagine how shocked the bank president was to learn that 14 of the locations asked me in one way or another to wait, call back, or return at a different time to see the "person who could help." Most of the time, the reason they couldn't assist me was because one person is "in charge of" that task in the smaller locations. If that particular banker was out of the office on an appointment or at lunch, the branch didn't have a plan in place to handle my impromptu visit. In their defense, these were very small communities in a rural area of Wisconsin. It must be quite uncommon for a new client to walk into the bank with this type of request. However, the solution is so simple and would cost so little.

All that was needed to resolve this issue was some additional training to handle the inquiries when the person who could open the account was unavailable at the moment of arrival. This could be accomplished with a simple one-sheet or low-cost brochure outlining the most popular accounts. At the very least, the staff person could have asked for my name and contact information with a promise of immediate follow-up when the staff person returned. Or, if it meant the difference between capturing a client and not, would it be possible to go all the way up the chain of command until reaching a person in charge who could make things happen, even if it was the bank president?

Secrets of an Undercover Shopper

Secret-Shopping Success Stories

Third-place winner: Sure-fire techniques for easier sales conversion

During a delightful secret-shopping tour, we were hired to visit retail stores in a well-known tourist community. One of the shops registered for the event was a boutique gift store filled with decorative dry flowers, vases, and knick-knacks. Upon entering with a friend, we browsed leisurely. At one point, I stopped to envy a large vase up on a high shelf and not easy to get down. This is often the setup I use when undercover shopping in retail. I asked the clerk if she could tell me how much the vase was off the top of her head without having to get it down. What I am looking for with inquiries like this is the level of helpfulness and level of irritation the employee shows when presented with a request that is inconvenient. She did

...process perfection is the key to moving a tire-kicker to an investor!

great, and I simply said, "Oh, that's a good price, I really like that vase. I'll think about it." Then I moved to the back of the store out of her sight for another 10 minutes. My hope was that when I returned, she would offer to get it down for me if I hadn't found something I liked better.

Was I ever surprised when I came around the corner to the front counter and the vase was not only down from its high perch, it was beautifully placed in a tissue-filled paper box with a lid and a shopping bag nearby. All I had to do was inspect it more closely and say yes, and it would be a done deal. She could not have done a better job of setting this up for an easy sales conversion. I did not feel pressured at all; in fact, she said, "Don't feel like you have to buy it, but I thought it would be easier for you to decide if you saw it up close." She was right. Plus, the packaging itself was so beautiful that it added to the emotional aspect of nodding yes.

Funny thing about secret shopping: Sometimes we find ourselves real buyers. That vase came home with me that day and I wasn't even in the market for decorative accents! Well done!

Secrets of an Undercover Shopper

Second-place winner: Process perfection!

A dental consultant association requested that I secret-shop 100 of the members who were registered for the annual meeting. The agreed-upon assignment was that my shoppers would present as an office manager of a three-doctor dental office in Northern Illinois in need of consulting work. The goal was to see how well they moved a tire-kicker to an invested client. With the help of my dentist, I was able to use his website and contact numbers as my façade to accurately access the entrepreneur's ability to chase a lead and close a deal. Overall, they were some of the best examples I've ever had in solid sales processes.

My most noteworthy consultant was one who did the following without hesitation or hiccups. She answered the phone promptly, listened intently instead of taking over the call, and responded to all of my questions patiently and slowly in a linear fashion, which is so important to information seekers. She was clear on how she could help, handled price objections liked a skilled professional, and offered free resource materials and shipped them out immediately. She followed up one week later as agreed and made sure to ask for the sale each time we spoke.

Whether you are a business owner like my case study or you are a team member responsible for moving an interested buyer to a committed one, process perfection is the key to moving a tire-kicker to an investor!

First-place winner: "Dog with a Bone" award

A bank hired us to secret-shop 10 of their branch locations that were in the middle of a campaign for new customers. A direct-mail postcard was sent to their target market stating that a special gift basket was available to anyone who opened up a new account during a certain time period. Those in charge of hiring me placed me into the system under my secret-shopper name and provided me with a postcard that I could use to help create the illusion of a real potential customer.

Most of the personal bankers I met on this tour did a wonderful job of talking with me, but they fell short when it came time for the ask. They couldn't convert the conversation to the point of opening the account, and I left time and time again with the undecided phrase, "I will think about it and get back to you."

Except for one banker. She was so exceptional at her sales techniques that she got me all the way to the point of the sale where I would need to provide a photo ID to open the account. When she asked for my street address, I froze. It was the first time a banker had gotten this far in the process without me pulling the rip cord. I didn't quite know how to gracefully escape, so I just blurted out a house number from a previous residence I had in another city years before. She paused, not recognizing the street name, and asked me where that was located. Again, feeling I was about to be caught, I said, "Oh, it's in the new subdivision north of town." She accepted that answer with a hint of skepticism and we continued on. Phew! ... at least that is what I thought at the time. When she got to the point of asking for a photo ID to open the account, I faked that I had foolishly forgotten my license in another purse and I would go get it and come back. We left on great terms and I gave her amazing reviews on her report with plans to give her an award at the reveal program.

But that's not the best part of the story.

On the day of the event when I presented her award, she came forward with a scowl and visible agitation toward me. On occasion, people have felt duped after being shopped, and I assumed that was the case with "Beth." Her boss asked if he could take the mic for a moment and tell the ending to the story. I had no idea where this was headed, so, with great hesitation, I surrendered control of the program. It turns out that when I had not returned that afternoon as promised, she was so dedicated to giving me the free gift that at 5 p.m. she punched out for the day and drove around for 45 minutes looking for a house address that does not exist in her town! Everyone was laughing and applauding her efforts, and eventually—after a profuse apology on my part—she gave me a smile.

I changed up her award from honorable mention to a special shout-out that still continues today: the "Tenacity Award," for having the tenacity of a dog with a bone. Well done! (And, "Beth," if you are reading this and recognize your story, I still feel bad for such a nasty game of hide-and-seek!)

What We've Learned from Years of Secret Shopping

After years of secret shopping, I started to see common denominators among those who received below-average scores. While not all the changes we suggested to our secret-shopping clients fell into the low-cost category, many of them did. They were simple—although not easy—"10¢" changes that could have made a big impact. But when I shared the results and recommendations with those in command, the reaction was generally a nodding of understanding and then a hesitation to take action. Other than agreeing to point out to staff the areas that could benefit from improvement, it didn't seem they had resources to train the change. Based on that, I decided to create The Guest Encounters™, an online video

...be ready for "showtime, go time, all the time!

training tool that includes 30 videos on topics related to customer service and staff development. It pulls all of the lessons we have learned from secret shopping, including the common errors and oversights, and puts them together in one spot along with tips and tools to stop them from happening in your organization. Many of them are shared in this book. However, many people learn even better from video education than from reading text.

Visit www.GuestEncounters.com to learn more.

There are two of these "10¢" concepts we learned about during secret shopping that your team can implement immediately with zero cost while providing the biggest benefit to your service levels. I am extremely confident that if the only thing you accomplish after reading this book is to consistently do the following two actions, along with the Big 7 of Service, your rave reviews will appear, and repeat business will occur. How do you create walking billboards of positive customer comments? Read on!

Secrets of an Undercover Shopper

1. Showtime mindset

Consider a theater in which the actors waiting behind the curtain do not get along well. There may be conflict or stress, but when they step on stage, they have lines to say and roles to play in order to give the audience an enjoyable experience. You'll never observe an actor step out of character, look out into the audience, and say, "Hey, you think my co-worker's a nice guy? You have no idea what he's *really* like." It simply would not happen in the theater.

The same should be true for business, but it isn't always. How often do we tell the customer things that happen behind the curtain that they don't need to know? Once the lights go on and the door is unlocked in your business, it's showtime. Show up in your costume (your business attire). Use the scripts you've been given (the right words at the right time for a desired result). And give your audience (your guest) the best possible experience, no matter how many times you've recited those lines or completed that task. I call this having a showtime mindset.

Think about what showtiming looks like in your organization. Remember, when the curtain rises, it is "go" time, whether you're feeling "on" or not. To provide a truly seamless guest encounter, you need to be ready for "showtime, go time, all the time!" Each guest expects—and deserves—a stellar performance.

On a recent flight from Chicago to Rapid City, South Dakota, I experienced firsthand the change in perception when an employee forgets the "all the time" part. Right before takeoff, the pilot came into the cabin and over the loudspeaker said, "Hey, everybody, I'm gonna tell you two jokes to which you will respond with laughter, groans, or boos. We will not take off until you have done this, got it?" he said in a laughing delivery. My seatmate, an obvious businessman en route to a big meeting, looked at me with an expression that said, "Did I just get on a Southwest flight by mistake?" The pilot continued to tell two jokes that were at about a fourth-grade level. We all groaned and then he said, "OK! Wheels up to Rapid City!" I have to admit the atmosphere in the cabin was lighter than usual for our short flight.

Secrets of an Undercover Shopper

I was already plotting in my head that I would do a Facebook Live video with the pilot after we landed to compliment him on his creative approach and debrief the fact that it had impacted us in a positive way. This would be great! However, when we landed, several of us were waiting on the jet bridge for our valet bags. I was also on the lookout for the funny pilot to exit the plane so I could make my request for a quick, fun interview.

Then it happened.

I witnessed right before my eyes a person who forgot that it is "Showtime, go time, all the time."

The passengers standing on the jet bridge were still audience members to this theater. But the pilot must have forgotten that. He met the replacement pilot just outside the door of the plane. They were standing right in front of me when I heard funny pilot say to replacement pilot, "Did they tell you about this plane? It's a piece of shit." He wasn't teasing, he was agitated. They exchanged a few other sentences, shook hands, and parted ways.

The conversation he needed to have with his work colleague should have taken place "behind the curtain," meaning outside our earshot. My confidence in the airline goes down when they put me on a plane that the pilot doubts, and my applause of the pilot goes away when he pulls back the curtain too far.

Every behavior matters, especially the ones that take place on stage. You might not always feel like being funny or patient or courteous, but your guests don't really care how you feel. It's your job to make them feel like they have a front-row seat to the best service in the house.

2. Transitions matter

One area that receives the lowest scores when we conduct a customer service audit on a business is their ability to create smooth transitions. Imagine a track relay team. One runner has the baton. As he approaches the next runner, they stride in unison for several lengths. He then passes the baton without losing stride. Olympic-level runners have spent hours perfecting this transfer, because it can be the difference between winning a medal or going home empty-handed. What does this look like in a business setting?

Dropping the baton. Visualize a couple walking into a bank. They are greeted by a teller at a service window, and they explain that they want to see a loan officer about buying a car. They share the story of car shopping with the teller, who nods, smiles, and listens. However, when she phones the personal banker, she only says, "Somebody's here to see you."

A winning hand-off. The same couple enters the bank. A teller calls the personal banker and says, "I have a couple who would like to see you. Are you available?" She then escorts them to the office

...transfer of trust is important.

and makes a transition introduction: "Amy, I'd like you to meet Ted and Martha Brown, clients of ours, and they would like to talk to you about a car loan. Ted and Martha, this is Amy Thompson, one of our personal bankers, and she will be happy to provide the information you need."

If the teller is unable to leave the counter, then the same message can be communicated by phone without the formal introduction. When the personal banker comes out of the waiting area to greet the clients, she needs to communicate that the baton was passed. "Good afternoon, Mr. and Mrs. Brown. I'm Amy Thompson, your personal banker. Please follow me to my office." Once in the confidential space, she continues, "Kate tells me you're interested in getting a car loan, and I'm happy to help you with this." A successful transition positively impacts the guest encounter.

Another successful transition occurs in an optometrist's office following an eye exam. Instead of just bidding the patient goodbye and walking out of the room, the doctor escorts the patient to the optician. Since this is the team member who will help the patient select and purchase the eyewear, a transfer of trust is important. The doctor should say something like, "Ms. Patient, allow me to introduce you to Ellie. She's the expert around here on finding the perfect frame for the shape of your face. You are in good hands. We'll see you next year for your annual checkup. OK?"

Telephone transfers. Transitions by phone are also important. Have you ever called somewhere knowing that the first person who picks up is not going to be the person to answer the question you have? In order to transfer you to the right person, they ask you what you need. After you tell the long version of your issue, they say, "One moment. Let me connect you." Then you have to start all over.

Better service would sound like this: "After getting enough information from you, I'm going to call and give a summary to the staff person who's going to help you." After the staff person makes a smooth transition, the next person in line to take care of you would say, "Mrs. Larson, this is Robin in the billing department. Mary tells me that you have a question on your last statement. I have it pulled up here on my screen. Let me just confirm that I have the right account, and we'll see where that extra charge is coming from." That is a smooth transition.

Put Transitions in Place

Put a professional transition plan in place using these starter steps:
1. Introduce yourself.
2. Recap the situation in one to two sentences.
3. Choose words that create the expectation that the next part of your guest's experience will be positive.
(See Positive Positioning in the next chapter.)
4. Give a head nod of confirmation that the exchange is accurate.
5. Smile and make your departure.

Sound simple? It is! Just follow the steps.

Also, be gentle with your internal customers, even when they are passing a baton that you don't necessarily want to accept. A task request that comes at an inopportune time and recurring requests from a challenging customer are examples of tough transfers. If you bite off the head of the co-workers responsible for passing you the baton, you are creating a stressful work environment. Learn to process your stress in a manner that does not abuse your co-workers. Train yourself to politely thank them for the information, for helping to get the baton in your hand in a professional manner, and for helping carry the load. A supportive work environment makes the day more pleasant for everyone, including you.

However, if your team is not accustomed to a "showtime" culture or proper transitions, you may need to have a few practice sessions. Work to find the right sentences to use and make sure that every team member understands his or her role in the teamwork and the hand-off. Soon it will be second nature in your service process, and the positive customer-service reviews will increase.

Discussion Questions

How would your team score if secret shopped today?

What recent actions of your team would be award winning?

Are there recent encounters that included a missed opportunity?

What feedback system is currently used in your organization, and is it effective?

Have you reviewed the "transition points" in the flow of your business to identify what adjustments would be beneficial to your guests?

The Power of Positive Positioning:
Setting Up the Right Service Expectations

If I had to pick a single phrase to summarize the secret behind providing superior service, it would be "never disappoint the guest." *After you have covered all of the basics of service, what will it take to exceed the expectations of the customer in order to achieve outstanding reviews, feedback, and recommendations? Do you have a mindset of positive positioning?* This concept can be used by every person reading this book, regardless of your product, service, or position. Once you have set the expectation bar high for a good experience, do not disappoint.

Don't Let Them Down

A turning point in the early years of my speaking business occurred when a client was trying to choose between me and two other presenters. This is common in the field of speaking. They narrow it down to a three-pack of professionals who all fit the criteria for the job, and then a committee votes on which speaker they like best. Sometimes the decision is based on video samples, the strength of the referral, or just a gut feeling. Many times, I don't even know why I was or wasn't chosen. It's one of the most vulnerable parts of the job.

Anyway, I really wanted this particular contract, and I decided to be a little bolder in my word choice than I had been in previous years when finding myself in this situation. As the sales call was wrapping up, I said to the potential client, "If your committee decides to go with one of the other two speakers over me, what would be the reason for that choice?" I must have caught her off-guard because there was a long pause, and then she said, "I'm really not sure. I think you are the best one for our needs." I didn't plan in advance to say the next sentence. I hadn't practiced it or role-played it with a colleague to make sure it sounded good. It just popped out from a place of pure sincerity. I replied with a smile (which can be heard over the phone), "We'll that's great to hear. I promise that if I am chosen, I won't disappoint you." She called back later that afternoon and said I was unanimously chosen by the committee because they needed someone they could count on to deliver the objectives and her gut was telling her I was the right choice for this.

I am familiar with the other two speakers who were up for the engagement, and they too would have done a wonderful job. I truly believe the main reason I got the nod was because I put their concern into words. It's the biggest fear meeting planners have, no matter what the event. They need to find someone who will do what they ask and not let them down. I was inadvertently using specific, positive words to address their concerns or objectives, which I refer to as positive positioning. And it worked.

Twenty-two years later, I am still saying something similar in the close of my emails. When a customer has decided I am the one they want to contract with, I send a booking agreement along with a very concise thank-you in the body of the email. The last sentence reads, "Thank you so much for your confidence in my work. I will not disappoint you." It is interesting how many people will echo those words back at me after an event. They say things like "You were right, you didn't disappoint" or "Yep, that was exactly what we wanted."

I believe the reason I even thought to use those particular words, "I won't disappoint you," came from a story I had heard years before. I was preparing for a presentation for a large hospital system. I asked the critical-care nurse supervisor what she wanted her staff to hear during my talk. She responded, "I want you to reinforce the point I make to each and every one of them during their orientation. I tell them, 'There will be a day when one of your patients may be spending his last day on earth with you. Do not disappoint him.'"

The Power of Positive Positioning

What an impactful statement—and it cost me nothing! And even though it is unlikely that your customers are spending their last day on earth with you, the mentality of the statement is the basis of this chapter. Her dedication to never-ending superior service was visible in everything this nurse did at work, from her climb up the ladder to her focus on training the next new class of nurses. I was moved by it and tried to find ways to incorporate the mindset into my own business.

Positive Positioning Starts with Identifying the Noteworthy Asset

Positive positioning statements are usually based on building up the experience of being noteworthy. For example, I made a reservation at a spa. At the end of the phone conversation, the receptionist said, "Just wait until you see our infinity pool and our power shower." She spoke with such enthusiasm that I couldn't wait to get to the place. When I got there, it did not disappoint. The infinity pool and the power shower were, in fact, fantastic! This spa is a place I would recommend again. She set that bar of expectation.

On the other hand, just recently I made an appointment at a spa that was inside a brand-new five-star hotel. It had only been open one week, and the newly trained staff member said, "Come early and take advantage of time in our Alpenglow Fireplace Lounge." This sounded amazing! Taking him up on his suggestion, I arrived at the spa an hour before go time with great anticipation. The word "alpenglow" means the rosy light of the setting sun seen on high mountains. This spa is located in Denver with a view of the Rocky Mountains, so the name is perfect, but the expectations were set a little too high. The room was nice: comfortable lounge chairs, unlimited coconut water, and steaming-hot eucalyptus-scented washcloths for the eyes. However, there was nothing remotely connected to a sun, and the fireplace was a small electric fake flame with a vent that rattled the entire time. I think the room would have gotten a fairly good rating from me if they hadn't teed it up to be something more than they delivered.

Listen for Hesitation Points

Another way to use positive positioning is to listen for hesitation points in the buyer's communication and balance them with accurate praise. For example, an assistant during an initial call is trained to listen for hurdles in order to address them. If the client pauses when it's time to schedule a financial-planning consultation, the administrative assistant might say something like, "What I like about working with Sally is that she's really honest with her recommendations. She will show you all the options and not be pushy in her advice. Clients really appreciate that about her." If you are a solopreneur and you answer your own phone, it may be hard to say how great you are without sounding a little conceited, right? Consider using phrases such as "I'm proud of..." or "Many of my clients comment on..."

To set an expectation of a good experience and create the image you desire, generate a list of specific things to compliment about your organization, your people, your product, and your service. Try recruiting your co-workers or boss to help; or, if you're a solopreneur, ask a few trusted clients or friends. If you can't come up with a list, well, then you've uncovered a bigger issue.

Once you have your list, develop sentences that work to communicate your positives in a way that feels comfortable. For example, "He's a great doctor" could be "Our patients often tell us Dr. Foster is so easy to talk to."

...look at your marketing materials as though seeing them for the first time.

The statements, of course, need to be truthful and accurate. Once you fine-tune the language, even simple words can make a difference. Adverbs like *definitely, absolutely,* and *certainly* are great examples of response words with great impact.

Next, look at all of your marketing materials and review them as though seeing them for the first time. This includes not only your printed promotional materials, statements, letters, and thank-you cards, but also your website, email newsletters, social-media profiles, and even your email signature line.

How do you look in print? Is your message clear and easy to understand? Perhaps you made the mistake of making copy after copy of a document without returning to the original. Now when you look at your printed materials, they're faded or maybe even crooked on the paper. What about your online presence? When was the last time it was updated? Does it accurately represent you or the brand you represent? Do the words you've chosen set the right expectations for your guests? Are you missing opportunities to use positive positioning statements? Put your findings from this exercise into action to improve your positioning. It's possible that making changes to the brand's image is not within the boundaries of your job description. If that's the case, I encourage you to share this chapter with those who can activate the change sequence.

Dealing with Difficult People

It's inevitable that sooner or later you will disappoint a guest. It could be a misunderstanding, a time you fell short on a promise, or a flat-out mistake that could have been avoided. No matter what the reason, being prepared and learning some specific skills can help you better handle the situation. Think of the angry person as a block of ice. In fact, sometimes their body language even looks firm and solid like a block of ice. Your job is to use your own body language and words to help defrost the situation. If it's done right, you may even be able to get to a smile and a thank-you.

While there's no secret formula for defusing every situation, I've found a combination of these 12 steps helpful in making bad situations better. Please note that the steps do not have to be done in order. Use them mix-and-match style for the particulars of each situation where you encounter an angry person.

1. Stay calm

Most of the time, as frontline staff, you take the brunt of angry customers. It's instinctive to flee or fight when faced with a tense situation, but neither is the right answer. You must practice staying calm by taking slow, deep breaths while concentrating on maintaining eye contact.

2. Stop, look, listen, lean forward, be responsive

If possible, move agitated customers from your counter area to a private room or adjacent hallway. Stop all other activity and concentrate on what the person is telling you. Body language is an important tool for showing a customer you are serious about resolving the issue. Nodding, eye contact, and note-taking are all excellent modes of silent communication. Most important, keep quiet. If you interrupt, the person will assume you are not listening and often feel the need to start over again. Patiently listen to the whole story. When the customer has clearly finished, you may respond. When it's your turn to speak, begin with agreement. Even if this requires really digging to uncover some common ground, do so. Obviously, you are not going to agree with false statements, but you could reply with "I'm glad you brought this to our attention. I'd like to help solve this problem."

3. Accept the anger

Try not to take the demonstration of anger personally. Most of the time people do not know how to express displeasure pleasantly—I suppose that's an oxymoron. Some people assume they will get better results with rage than with polite dialogue.

By the way, if *you* are ever the angry customer in a place of business, this is a great step to use in your favor. Help the other person by saying in a sincere, pleasant tone, "I know it isn't your fault, but I'm very upset about this situation and I hope you can help me." This often works better than berating an innocent team member.

4. Accept responsibility

Never say, "There's nothing I can do." As we learned earlier, that statement is like gasoline on a fire. Although it may range from simply gathering facts to solving the problem, there's always *something* you can do. If you are a member of a team, then all the work done for the customer is a reflection of the overall quality. Remember that the majority rules. If most of the staff people with whom customers come into contact are surly or unsatisfactory, they assume all the workers are the same. All for one, and one for all is the way a successful office should operate. That sometimes includes taking responsibility for the actions of a co-worker and working with the guest to help resolve their problem.

5. Refer to the proper person

As soon as you have determined the best person to solve the problem, explain this to the customer. Choose your words carefully: "Mr. Smith, the best person to help you understand your current bill is Melanie, our staff member in charge of accounts receivable. Let me explain your needs to her and she will be happy to talk with you right away."

These two short sentences carry a bundle of information to the customer. Let's break it down:

- "Mr. Smith"—use the customer's name.
- "understand your current bill"—identify the problem as you see it.
- "Melanie, our staff member in charge of accounts receivable"—identify the person who can solve the problem.
- "will be happy to"—indicate that you're not bothered in any way by the request.
- "let me explain your needs to her"—remove the need for the customer to rehash the issue.
- "she will talk with you right away"—indicate responsiveness.

6. Ask questions

This step reminds me of the old saying to "gather your facts." It is a fundamental rule by which we should all live. There is always more to the story. By asking questions, you can uncover hidden facts to help you put the puzzle together.

Ask questions like:
- "What were you told?"
- "When did you call?"
- "Do you know to whom you spoke?"

7. Restate the problem and ask for confirmation

If you have successfully followed the previous steps to determine the problem, you should have a basic understanding of the complaint. Now is the time to summarize the story. Remember to present the recap from the customer's perspective. In other words, if you know a part of the story is not accurate, you can insert such bridges as "and you feel, Mr. Smith" or "your impression was."

8. Respond visibly

Be careful to have the right facial expression. The easiest way to achieve this step is simply to nod. Try not to be too defensive, even if you're the cause of the complaint. Avoid being too smiley. Serious, professional, and focused are the best traits to show. The customer wants to see you take some kind of action in response to their complaint. For example, if a customer brings in an item that is broken, take it from them and look at it while they explain. Or if the person is angry about a bill and thrusting it in your face while ranting, take the paper and look it over while occasionally looking up and nodding.

9. Agree

I'm not asking you to agree with a customer who may be insulting, rude, or wrong. Agreeing in this case means to understand or empathize. A well-known, time-tested technique for dealing with a complaint is the "Feel, Felt, Found" method. "I understand how you feel, Mr. Smith. I would have *felt* that way too. What we have *found* is that if we (insert solution here), it seems to help."

10. Develop solutions

This is my favorite step. It is often the turning point in defrosting an angry person. Start tossing out suggestions to solve the problem. If it's a simple scenario, one solution often suffices. Other times, multiple options are necessary. Say something like, "We can do (insert option A) or we can do (insert option B); which of these is best for you?" Then stop talking and wait for a response. You often will find that the customer will choose one of the options provided, and you are well on your way to solving this situation. When faced with a customer who will not respond to any of your suggestions, try this statement: "What can we do to make this situation better?" Occasionally the reply is a third option you may not have thought of but can easily provide.

11. Exceed expectations

We refer to this as "Replace Plus 1." That means not only do we try to solve the problem, but we also add a touch of appreciation with it. Adding a special touch or offer that is applicable to your industry is a great place to start. This applies when your organization is clearly "in the wrong" and needs to make up for a poor decision or unfortunate situation. For example, while you're staying in a hotel there is a loud party in the room next to you. After you complain to the management, they not only move you, but also give you dollars off your stay or extra reward points.

12. Personalize

Simply remembering to use a person's name in the conversation and, when appropriate, adding a tone of familiarity can be a "10¢" turning point when dealing with an extremely irate person. Once, I dealt with an enraged patient. I tried everything to calm him. I was speaking in a very formal, professional tone and referred to him as Mr. Anderson throughout the conversation, but none of the steps were working to calm him down. Finally, when he appeared to be finished, I started my first sentence with his first name, and I said it in a tone like we were old friends chatting over the fence in our backyards. "So, Joe, what am I gonna have to do to improve this situation?" Immediately he seemed to relax a little, probably because of the personal touch. He came up with a simple suggestion, one I hadn't thought of. I agreed that his idea was a great compromise and he seemed satisfied. I'm not sure I would have come to that point without using step 12—bringing a personal tone into the conversation.

After enough practice, this 12-step approach to dealing with angry customers becomes second nature. There isn't a hard-and-fast rule on how to use the steps. Many times, I find myself using step 12 first. Use the knowledge you've learned in this book about energy levels, body language, and word choice to read the guest and determine the best first step.

The Power of Positive Positioning

Upgrade your words, message, and image. See what a difference positive positioning makes to your guest encounter. Then go beyond expectations by never disappointing the buyer.

I think we likely agree that customer service is often common sense. However, if we leave common sense to chance, there is the possibility it fails in execution. The good news is that the steps outlined in this book are easy to accomplish. All it takes is focus and effort from you and your team. Instead of getting stuck on the major changes you could make, I encourage you to start with a simple thing you can do—*The 10¢ Decision*—and prove to yourself how small change pays off big.

Discussion Questions

Is your company ever guilty of building something up to be bigger than it really is?

Do you have things you offer that you haven't bragged about enough?

Can you generate a list of specific things to compliment about your organization, your people, your product, and your service?

Do you have a training program in place to help staff practice how best to deal with angry guests?

Do you track complaints and make a plan for adjustments when a common thread develops that causes angry customers?

Epilogue

Dear Team Member,

I encourage you to honestly self-assess your ability to deliver the strategies I've described in this book. If you are struggling day-to-day, it may be time to invest in personal training or coaching. Learning how to thrive in challenging environments is one of the hardest things to do, and getting help can make all the difference in the outcome.

> *Please take the time to flip over the book and read it from the other side.*

A very small portion of the text is duplicated, so there are many more ideas in the other half. Plus, to understand those to whom you report, it's important to think about their challenges and see things through their goggles as well. I am confident it will be worth your time and effort in order to pull all of this together.

Final Thought

I had the privilege of working for years under the mentorship of many doctors and a stellar management team. It is through their unrelenting training that my entire professional career was formed. Providing superior customer service was so important to me that I, in turn, was asked to begin teaching others our secrets. I didn't know at the time that it would become my life's work as a professional speaker and trainer. There isn't a topic I feel as much passion about as I do service.

Please remember that every customer, client, patient, or patron who comes to you needs something. If you can fulfill that need while treating them like a treasured guest in your home, then every encounter can exceed expectations. Not because it cost a fortune to deliver the best, but because you are talented enough to carry out the small details involved in *The 10¢ Decision.*

Flip Time!

CPSIA information can be obtained
at www.ICGtesting.com
Printed in the USA
BVHW082334071019
560431BV00006B/316/P

the 10¢ decision

How small change pays off big

Leader Guide to Exceptional Service

About the Author

An entrepreneur, keynote speaker and author, Laurie Guest became known as a "go-to-resource" for customer service excellence during a successful career in the healthcare industry. In 1997, she channeled that expertise into Guest Enterprises, Inc., her own speaking and training company designed to inspire stellar customer service and help others create noteworthy guest experiences.

For more than two decades, she has shared her practical point of view on customer service and staff development to audiences across the country, blending real-life examples and proven action steps for improvement. Laurie is an award-winning columnist and the author of two books. With her latest, *The 10¢ Decision: How Small Change Pays of Big,* Laurie presents her most sought-after and impactful strategies to find and retain the best staff and highest-quality customers while delivering exceptional guest experiences.

A certified speaking professional, a designation held by less than 12% of speakers worldwide, Laurie lives in northern Illinois, where she is a wife, mother of two, lover of board games and a below-average cook.

Acknowledgements

My deepest thank you to the many trusted friends and colleagues who helped make this book a reality. You know the role you played. My appreciation runs deep.

Starting first with the team who made the book happen. My amazing editor, Jenn Woolson, who took a thousand-piece puzzle and assembled into a picture I am proud to share. Designer extraordinaire, Wendy Tritt, who always knows how to read my mind and then make it look good. Book retreat pal, Mary Byers, if it had not been for our writing retreat, I am not sure this book would have ever left the starting gate. And Lisa Trifone, the best public relations partner a writer could ask for.

Thank you to my mastermind buddies: Anna Liotta, John Sileo, Bill Stainton, Brian Walter, and Liz Weber for making me believe my words matter.

A special thank you for the regular check-ins from Lori Klinka and Kelly Swanson. You have the patience to listen to me process just about every thought I have, which is quite an undertaking.

As always, I need to thank my husband, Tom, for his never-ending support of my work. Our family is what matters most.

And finally, to all the clients and business owners who allowed me to interview them or use their organization as an example in the book, please let me take this time to say I am grateful.

Prologue

Dear Leader,

You've established a solid business and expected it to be bursting at the seams with customers by now—but it's not. You're confident that your products and services are on target with what your customer base desires, but still things aren't exactly the success you imagined them to be when you started your business or took over a leadership position in your organization.

I know you're challenged trying to figure out when and how to train your staff to deliver exceptional service. You are likely frustrated with staff turnover and inconsistent service delivery. You keep promising yourself to set time aside to figure out the components that will make it all work. But somehow, daily demands take over and you're forced to break the promise to yourself again and again to deal with this essential task.

Are you ready for a painless solution that can set your business on course for success overnight?

I bet your staff is ready. This book shares the guiding principles of customer service with proven techniques to attract and keep customers. One side is written for leaders and starts on the "back side" of the book, the direction you are reading now. But not all of the advice is the same-old, same-old service tips you've seen everywhere. I promise to share some fresh strategies to up your customer-service game to a whole new level—or, at the very least, you'll be reminded to actually implement what you already know. At the end of each chapter are questions that, when answered honestly, will lead to forward movement in your business and take you beyond the basics. But that part is up to you. If you read the book without

taking action, the insights won't make any impact on your service level or your bottom line. Taking action is the only thing that creates results.

It's the Little Things That Matter

Think about a product or service you were drawn to and consider whether the way it was packaged or presented is what first attracted your attention. I've ordered a flight of martinis because of the tiny, fancy, multi-colored glasses they were served in. My friend ordered a very expensive appetizer in an elite club because the caramelized bacon chunks came with a cotton-candy stick. And let's be honest, the best reason to order saganaki is because the server lights it on fire tableside and yells, "Opa!" Without that show, it's really just fried cheese. (Not to discount the amazing value of fried cheese.)

My favorite example of how packaging can make a difference revolves around bottled water. We all have little things in life that we're picky about. Me? I'm picky about water. That's right, I am a water connoisseur, which is cheaper than being a wine connoisseur.

As you can imagine, it bugs me when I check into a fancy five-star hotel and they want me to pay FOUR DOLLARS for a regular bottle of water. I mean seriously, for $350 a night, I ought to be getting a foot massage from a Chippendales dancer.

My point is that this water costs very little, and yet they can't throw one my way? Swanky hotel, and all I remember is the $4 bottle of water.

Now, let's pop into another hotel where I stayed. Moderately priced this time. Not fancy. I get to the room, parched and winded. I spot a mini-fridge with a sign that reads "Dear Valued Guest." (I love it that they put *my* last name on the sign.) "Please enjoy a complimentary bottle of water from the refrigerator."

It's likely those bottles of water cost the hotel only about 10¢ each when purchased by the truckload. And even though the quality level of the water wasn't anything memorable, by simply delivering it to me differently—in the fridge, and free—my perceived value was considerably higher.

Prologue

So why am I telling you all this? Why am I making a big deal out of a bottle of water? Because most of us in business don't realize that sometimes it's the 10¢ decision that can have the biggest impact.

If you really want to provide exceptional service and keep customers coming back, I suggest focusing on small changes. How small? It can be as simple as better word choices or a little extra add-on. But the key is, it doesn't have to cost your company much more than a dime.

> ...sometimes it's The 10¢ Decision that can have the biggest impact.

Are You Wondering Why Laurie?

What makes me an expert on the topic of customer service? How do I know the right combination of service components to help you make the 10¢ decisions to create the ultimate guest experience? It's because of my real-world entrepreneurial experience that started when I was just 5 years old. I grew up inventing new ideas that led to cash, and that was exciting to me.

What I know to be true about customer service is that many organizations think proper treatment of their clients is common sense and that training isn't an issue. Unfortunately, leaders often believe that if they hire good people, their employees will just *know* how to treat customers. WRONG. The basics must be taught, enforced, and reinforced to create the ultimate customer experience.

In this short, easy-to-read book, I share the insights I have gained in each phase of my working life. During every endeavor, I remained committed to providing great service to every customer/patient/ guest I encountered. I've also collected quite a few examples through the years that prove each of my points in a relatable fashion. In each chapter, you'll find a lesson that takes a deeper dive into the attributes that can help you achieve great reviews and success simply by improving your guest encounter points.

Prologue

Here's the Best Part!

I realized while writing this book that there are actually two different audiences who need this content. One is you, the leader, which could mean the business owner, C-suite member, training director, manager, or anyone in a leadership position who may need help identifying those small ideas that can make a big impact. The other is the team member, who is asked to deliver great customer service but may never have had any formal training in how best to treat customers. To make all of this work, you need an integrated approach. To help them, just flip the book over and encourage them to read it from the other direction. Those chapters speak to their needs and core issues. That's right, two books in one!

Also, it's not a bad idea to flip the book yourself and read the other half. It's filled with great stories and creative ideas that show how small changes can pay off big. You'll discover all sorts of ways to help make the 10¢ decision that could have a big impact on the customer experience that your business delivers.

Are you ready to get at it? Let's do this!

Create a Noteworthy Guest Experience:
Secrets to Making Every Encounter Memorable

Word of mouth is the best advertising—if what your customers have to say is positive. When you provide a guest with an experience so good that they want to share it with others, you've created the best referral possible. *How do you create and provide memorable encounters? Do you have a plan for turning your guests into walking billboards because their experience is so amazing that they must share it with others?* Deciding what constitutes a noteworthy experience for your guest is a great place to start, and it's a lesson I learned in first grade.

Secrets of the Sweet Corn Stand

When I was about 7 years old, my parents decided I was old enough to have a sweet corn stand. I grew up in Somonauk, Illinois, a small farming community about 60 miles west of Chicago. My dad was born there, as were the three generations of his family before him. Raising children in a small town had its advantages. The car could be left running with a kid in it and no one would think it was an unwise choice. We knew almost every person in town, and a helping hand was never farther away than a phone call. So, finding buyers for my well-reputed product was not hard. I remember my mom saying that the corner of Gage and Market streets, by the post office, would be the best spot. In a 1,300-person community, one could anticipate major foot traffic at this "heart of the village" intersection. One corner had our only gas station and across the street was the only grocery store. Mail, food, gas: the trifecta of small-town America.

Create a Noteworthy Guest Experience

So, with a pickup truck full of the finest ears of corn in the land, we parked on the corner. Mom set up a card table for me and a pile of brown paper sacks with a sign that I drew myself: "Baker's Dozen $2.50!" Now, I don't know who decided that two and half bucks was the going rate, but my product was definitely priced to sell. Those bags of 13 cobs were flying out from under my table so fast we couldn't keep up. While I was busy selling, my dad, my older brother, and a few helpers had taken the truck back to the farm to bring me another load.

Keep in mind that the sweet corn I was selling was harvested by hand. You find ears that are ripe enough to be picked, then you break them off the stalk with a swift twist of the wrist. It's actually pretty hard work. It's a detail I forgot when the truck rolled up with a second load of corn. By that point, I had already been sold out of inventory for well over 15 minutes and people were starting to line up down the block. Being the lippy, 7-year-old boss that I was, I exclaimed in an angry tone, "Can't you guys get this stuff here any faster? We're losing customers!"

What I learned that summer was that although our product was excellent and our prices were unbeatable, those weren't the only reasons for my sweet success. I learned an important lesson about making every encounter memorable. My parents insisted that I thank every customer for taking the time to stop by. I created a noteworthy experience with friendly banter, an extra ear of corn, and a great price—but then I took the opportunity to go one step further. I offered to carry the bag to the car for the seniors, and sometimes people would just pull up to the curb to exchange cash for corn and never have to get out of the car. In the big scheme of things, these were very small gestures but they all added up to a great impression.

Sure, there were plenty of other places in town to buy sweet corn, but I sold out day after day. Why? Because I didn't just rely on location to bring in buyers. I was taught how to stand out in my tiny marketplace by providing a noteworthy customer experience.

Value-Add vs. Extras That Count

Is there a difference between the concepts of "value-add" and "extras that count" when making offers to customers? Yes! There is a difference, albeit a subtle one. Simply put, a "value-add" is a feature or benefit that increases the actual worth of the product or service. An "extra" is an additional action that provides value to the experience or service level without changing the purchase itself.

For example, when a car dealership offers replacement windshield wipers every year on the purchase anniversary, that's a "value-add." The customer doesn't have to pay $10 for the product. When that same dealership offers coffee and doughnuts while you wait for your oil change, that is an "extra that counts." Some customers will care about the extras more than others. My neighbor, who doesn't eat the free doughnuts the car dealership offers, won't notice or care about that special touch. Instead, she might value their friendliness when they answer the phone or appreciate the quick run through the car wash that they do before they return your keys.

For businesses running on a tight margin, the no-cost extras are key and usually come down to their teams' soft skills, commonly known as customer service. It's interesting to me that when it comes to educational programming, "soft skills" are often deemed less valuable or far from cutting-edge. Maybe calling it something different could help change the mindset about the value. A soft skill is a personal attribute that enables someone to interact effectively with other people.

> " I suggest we call it "indispensable talent"... "

When you think about it, there isn't a skill that is more valuable than that, because if we can't connect with our buyers in a way that matters most to them, what type of loyalty can we hope to achieve? I suggest we start to call it "indispensable talent" instead of soft skills.

As a customer-service expert, I'm watching for amazing talent everywhere I go so I can observe, learn, and spread the word. I'm always on the lookout for those small gestures that make an impact on my experience and create memorable moments worth talking

about—those 10¢ decisions. Some stories I tell for years after they happen, and that makes me a walking billboard for that business.

A few years ago, I purchased a vacuum cleaner from a local, independent, family-owned store rather than the big-box options in town. After paying for the purchase, I leaned over to pick up the carton to carry it out. The clerk stopped me, hoisted the box up onto his shoulder and headed toward the door with me following empty-handed. I said, "Oh, you don't have to carry it out to my car!" He got a big smile on his face and said, "No problem, this is how we kick Walmart's ass." I've never forgotten that statement, because it is so true. I could have purchased a very similar item for a cheaper price at a discount place. Why did I do business with the smaller store? Because of their product knowledge and service level. The larger store would never have given me advice on the best machine to buy. I figured I was better off talking to the guy who sells nothing but vacuums. The small, extra move of carrying the heavy box out to my car and adding humor to the conversation created a memorable moment—a moment that cost the owner absolutely nothing.

Stand Out in Your Marketplace

Create a unique stamp on your marketplace by delivering a noteworthy guest experience with extras that count.

Think of a situation when you felt the customer service you experienced was worth talking about. Mine was at a bed-and-breakfast in Madison, Wisconsin, in 1990. It remains noteworthy to this day because of the superior service I received before, during, and after our stay.

The service was impressive, starting with the first call to book a room. A friend referred me, so when I called, I mentioned his name to the owner. She not only remembered my friend by name, but also complimented his wife. During the call, I mentioned that I was looking for a quiet getaway with a water view. At the conclusion of my initial call, she asked for our favorite beverages and if we had any food allergies.

When we checked in, the owner referenced my request for a view of the water before leading us to the top-floor suite overlooking

the lake. In our room, we found a welcome basket filled with our favorite beverages on ice, a variety of snacks, brochures of sights to see and shops to explore in town, a calendar of events, and a map of the area. *She remembered what was important and referenced it.*

What an amazing first impression! It is worth noting that the cost to her was minimal, yet the impact was major.

Impressive hospitality continued with room service. Before we went to our room for the evening, the innkeeper inquired when we would like breakfast delivered to our room. Room delivery meant we didn't have to go downstairs to make small talk with strangers—my least favorite thing about staying at a B&B. At 8:00 the next morning, we heard a light tapping on our door. The sweetest voice said, "Your breakfast is outside the door when you're ready." I opened the door to find a cart with fresh flowers and a taste-tempting display of breakfast food. *She found a way to give a slight twist to the regular routine of a B&B experience.*

After our stay, I received a handwritten note in the mail thanking us for our business and requesting that, if we had enjoyed our stay, she would love it if we would tell others about the little slice of heaven in Madison. That's what she called it. And that's how I felt about it. *She asked that the noteworthy experienced be shared.*

When you peel away the little things, it was just a bed-and-breakfast stay. It was the special "10¢" touches before, during, and after that made a huge impact. They are the reason I am still talking about it almost 30 years later.

What can you do in your business to up every guest experience to noteworthy? Are there things you once did that have somehow gone by the wayside? Is it time to dust off those ideas and bring them back? Here are a few "value-add" and "extras that count" experiences I've had recently:

- We have a local breakfast spot that gives us two doughnut oles on the side, free with every purchase.
- My car-service driver brings me my favorite coffee order and the *Chicago Tribune* and has every phone charger known to man.

- I travel a lot, and I regularly choose my hotel based on rewards points and the extras they offer, like fresh-baked cookies and free high-speed Wi-Fi. Those things matter.
- My bank offers one teller lane dedicated to mail services. Our post office is on the opposite end of town from my home, but the bank is less than half a mile away. When I need to send mail, I no longer have to drive to the other end of town.

Being Memorable Before, During, and After

In addition to deciding which value-adds and extras you can deliver, it's also helpful to take a look at what point during the guest experience the offer occurs. Brainstorm on what you can do before, during, and after guest encounters to create a noteworthy experience for the buyer.

Let's get some ideas started for you on how to implement value-adds and extras to your offerings.

Before the encounter (an "attraction action")

- Complimentary consultations (home décor, financial services, healthcare screenings)
- Gathering of information for customized encounters (a treat basket specific to guest upon arrival to a B&B, essential oils recipe pre-mixed for spa client, preferred beverage provided by limo service)
- Confirmation calls that go beyond the basics (calming nerves before a medical procedure, providing directions to difficult-to-locate buildings, creating rapport by answering questions in advance)
- Insider information on upcoming sales or after-hours access reserved for VIPs
- Building anticipation of the encounter through creative messaging

Create a Noteworthy Guest Experience

Best "before" example

While planning a family vacation to Denver, a friend had recommended The Curtis Hotel because of the clever themed décor. The location includes a 13th floor, which is rare among hotels because many people consider it to be bad luck. However, this hotel used that to their advantage and themed it the "Ghostbusters" floor. When I called to make a reservation, the on-hold recording was so memorable it increased my anticipation of a great visit. A deliberately spooky voice says, "Ask to stay on the 13th floor, if you dare." The recoding continues with other fun statements about a variety of floors.

By the time our trip arrived, the youngest member of our family was bursting with excitement for this stop. We even paid a little extra to get one of the themed rooms on the 13th floor! The uniqueness of the place continued after arrival, with an elevator that had a different recording related to the theme as it stopped on each floor. As the doors open on the 13th floor, Jack Nicholson's voice says the famous line from the movie "The Shining," "Heeere's Johnny!" The hotel was able to provide a fun and very memorable experience without a great expense on their part—or the guests'.

During the encounter (an upsell or "satisfaction-ensuring action")

- Catalog brands extending free shipping, free returns, or coupon codes for online savings
- Headphones with music options at the dental office
- Additional service with purchase (on-site tailoring at a boutique men's store or a makeup lesson with certain level of cosmetic purchase)
- Hotels that offer replacement of forgotten personal items like a toothbrush or razor
- Free childcare provided at stores, gyms, or vacation resorts and cruises
- Unique VIP access and special events

Best "during" example

Many years ago, a high-end, locally owned department store was a popular place in our area. The owner of the store, Beth Willey, was the third generation of her family to manage Henderson's department store. It had four floors and sat on the corner of the two main streets in our small town. She created a VIP event that was special. In the months leading up to Christmas, specific businesses in town were invited in for after-hours access to the entire store. Because our clinic had more than 100 female employees, we were a good target for this campaign.

One evening in the winter, she close d the store early on a Friday night and did a "special invitation-only" event. The only shoppers allowed in the doors from 6 to 9 p.m. were the members of our team. She served cookies, hot cocoa, and even wine, a liquid that always helps a buyer make better decisions. There was fun music playing throughout the beautifully decorated store and she had some things tagged as special buys. On top of that, we received a 25% discount off our entire purchase, even if the item was already on the sale rack. Discounts of this size in retail were almost unheard of during this era and certainly not offered at Christmas. Finally, her extras behind the hospitality included free gift wrapping and a personal-shopper service to help with wardrobe development well into the next year. What she accomplished with this one-of-a-kind experience was certainly noteworthy:

1. It was fun shop to with friends and work colleagues. Conversation was plentiful, and it even included calling out to each other from behind dressing-room curtains. Actually, one of my strongest memories of the event is the laughter and yelling out to each other from across the store, a behavior we would never engage in during normal business hours with strangers.

2. We felt like VIPs getting behind-the-scenes access and discounts not available to everyone in the community.

3. Beth held this event right after new inventory arrived, so next-season apparel was available in many sizes.

4. It was billed as an event where men were welcome too. Because she had male and youth clothing, and even a small housewares and bedding area, it was an inclusive experience for all members of our medical team, not just the women.

Not only were there great benefits for the customers, but setting up the event in this way also provided benefits to the owner. Beth had a loyal following of local buyers who waited for her event rather than travel 40 miles to our mall. She sold more product in one small block of time than she could have if each of us had shopped individually. In fact, many of my co-workers said the VIP event was the main reason they shopped in her store.

It was a "win-win" event. Isn't that what we all look for in business?

After the encounter (a "come back soon" action)
- Cell phone companies that offer post-purchase training
- "Store bucks" for a future purchase based on quantity of the day's sale
- Loyalty cards or points systems
- Software products providing a hotline number for installation questions or problem-solving
- Carry-out service or curbside pickup
- "Shop again soon" incentives like 20% off a purchase in the next 14 days

Best "after" example
One creative idea I spotted more than 15 years ago was at a local gift and crafts store. If a shopper left without making a purchase, the clerk at the register would hand them a coupon that was professionally designed and printed. It read:

> *Thank you for visiting us!*
> *We are so sorry you were unable to find what you were looking for today. Your visit to our store was greatly appreciated! Please take this coupon as a gift for just coming by. Bring it on your next visit. It's worth $1.00 off your purchase of $5.00 or more!*

Create a Noteworthy Guest Experience

When researching for this book, I made a surprise visit to the store and spoke with the owners. I think I caught them a bit off-guard when I whipped out one of these coupons, which had been hibernating in a file folder in my office for more than a decade. They smiled when I showed it to them like it was a photo of an old friend found in a memory box. They confirmed that the "come-back buck coupon" was a successful campaign for many years. They tracked the utilization and found it profitable. But over time it faded away, to be replaced by a new idea. Some years back, they left the craft store franchise they were part of and rebranded the store with a new name and a new look. As they were sharing their story, I remembered they'd had a contest where community members could submit an idea for the new store name. I teased them that the name I had suggested had been overlooked, but that the contest itself was a noteworthy idea. You may not be in a position to rename your business, but do you have a product or service for which you could run a contest for naming rights? A special brew of coffee, a cupcake, or even a service? This is a creative "10¢" way to get attention and involvement in your community.

"Sweet Earth" was the chosen winner of the naming contest, and the store's goal is to bring customers high-quality products at fair, affordable prices. The coupon was replaced with the "Go Green, Save Green" bag. This unique program gives customers who bring in the store's reusable bag a 10% discount every day on all their purchases, even the ones that don't fit in the bag! Each year, they add more earth-friendly products, made in the United States. Sweet Earth has been voted "Best Place for a Gift" in our county by area residents, and in 2010 it was named "Small Business of the Year" by the local chamber. The reason? Multiple examples of noteworthy customer experience.

Don't Be Shy About Pointing Out Value-Add Offers

Don't make the mistake of failing to let your guests know when you offer something of value. I'm aware of an attorney and an accountant who often choose to reduce their fee a little bit as a courtesy to certain clients. For example, if the bill is supposed to be $850, they might mark it down to $700. However, when they send the invoice, it just reads $700, with no mention of the discount. When "Agnes" is at the beauty shop the next day, she might complain to all who will listen about how high her bill was and share her level of dissatisfaction.

> ...let your guests know when you offer something of value.

But if the invoice reflects the discount, her messaging is more likely to mirror the same level of appreciation. She will instead share with others how nice her attorney is because he gave her a little discount that brought down her bill. Or, at the very least, she will not become a walking negative billboard.

Show the fee for the service of $850 with a single line through it and $700 written next to it. Then underneath, provide a short explanation for the reduction—*courtesy discount* or whatever the reason might be. The same is true if you're adding extras but not letting the client know you've done something special—it defeats the purpose.

When you make it a point to be on the lookout for the value-added services you encounter in your personal life, you'll find it easier to formulate new ideas for your own business. Examples are everywhere of small, "10¢" offerings that make a big difference. When you are creative in adding value before, during, and after your guest experiences, you'll open up many opportunities to build lasting relationships and repeat business.

It's vital, of course, to carefully process the cost benefits of initiating any of these value-added products and services—even those that appear to be low-cost extras—before you execute any new policy. For example, a jewelry-shop owner thought adding a small box of

chocolates with every order was a nice touch. That's until she realized that over a 12-month period, she had added a significant cost to her packaging without truly impacting the guest's experience. She may have been better off adding each customer to the shop's "members only" list, which entitled them to free cleanings or early notice on special sales, instead of investing in the expensive chocolate.

Deliver a noteworthy experience, make extras count, and provide value-added benefits. Dig deep to stand out in your marketplace. Finally, when you notice that you've made an impression on your buyer, don't be shy. Ask them to post a picture, post a comment, or review your business on social media. Noteworthy experiences are the easiest way to get new and repeat customers.

Create a Noteworthy Guest Experience

Discussion Questions

How do you currently create and provide memorable encounters?

Are there things you once did that have somehow gone by the wayside that you should consider bringing back?

What can you create as value-add for your guests before, during, and after the encounter?

Are your guests aware of all the extras and value-adds you offer? If not, what are some ways you can let them know?

Have you evaluated the value-adds and extras you offer? Are they worth the cost?

Packaging That Gets Noticed:
Get Creative to Better Position Your Product

Just as your team members make an impression on your guests, so does your packaging. In this case, packaging refers to so much more than a physical container for a product. It's the creative branding, bundling, and bling your business brings to every guest interaction—from the sign on your door to the way you say "thank you." *Do you have a strategy for naming and positioning your products and services? Is there room for creative packaging in your industry that can set you apart in the marketplace?* Finding clever ways to be unique can have a huge impact on how your goods and services are perceived and consumed.

The Pitfalls of the Painted Pencils

The sweet corn stand was my most profitable adolescent endeavor. Mostly because I didn't have to pay any expenses or labor costs! I had a team who was determined to help me succeed, and they were willing to endure my bossy behavior. Because the income was so good and the praise from the townspeople so fantastic, I caught the entrepreneurial bug, and it has never left me.

By the summer after fifth grade, I was geared up to invent an idea that others weren't already doing. My friend Joan and I decided through hours of brainstorming and discussion that we could paint pencils and sell them.

You're probably wondering, *Why pencils?*

Our parents were golfers, and Joan and I spent a lot of time at the country club messing around in the clubhouse and searching the

out-of-bounds areas looking for lost golf balls. In hindsight, it would have made a lot more sense to set up a station at the first tee and sell used golf balls rather than offering painted pencils. I could even picture a day when we could expand our offerings to include bottled water and bags of chips for those who didn't have time to stop for food between nines. But that didn't occur to us then.

We must have figured that because those little yellow pencils were so prevalent at the course, they must be important. We helped ourselves to an entire box of them conveniently located in the small mailbox near the first tee. For those of you unfamiliar with the game of golf, it's common for golf courses to put extra score cards and pile of 3.5-inch pencils near the first tee so those who may have forgotten to get the supplies at the clubhouse can grab them there instead of going all the way back. These are free for paid golfers. They are not meant to be swiped by little girls with big ideas. Let me be clear—at the time, we didn't realize we were stealing.

We opened for business on Fourth of July weekend, so it was obvious that pencils with red, white, and blue stripes would be timely. Using tempera paints, we carefully applied a stripe of each patriotic color on a third of the pencil. It was a messy, tedious job, but we were confident they would sell, so it was worth the effort.

However, two steps in our process were flawed. First, we allowed the pencils to dry overnight on sheets of newspaper, and we were surprised in the morning to find them stuck to the newspaper. We were disappointed when some of the paint peeled off when we picked them up. Second, because we used water-soluble paint, it came off easily in sweaty hands. (Incidentally, all golfers have sweaty hands in July.) We were not deterred, though, and off to sell we went.

What happened next won't surprise you.

Although everyone was kind to us, no one needed or wanted our product. Zero sales.

Across the street from the golf course were the fairgrounds, where the annual fireworks show took place. My friend convinced me we should try selling the pencils there. To this day, I still can't understand

why we thought anyone would need a pencil in the dark. But we set off with our wares to try again.

Of course, we were disappointed when no one was willing to pay for our great invention.

> "...to set yourself apart, you have to do something different..."

It all could have turned out differently if we knew at that age how much packaging and naming matters. What if we had convinced our moms to buy us two dozen mini-flashlights and put them in lunch sacks decorated to look like flags. Add a few mini candy bars and tiny notepads to go with the painted pencil and sell the kit as a "Fireworks Show Activity Bag" for kids to use while they waited for the show to start. No doubt, we would have sold out!

What Joan and I didn't know that summer is what any seasoned salesperson will tell you: It's all about the bling. Sure, you have to have substance too. There's no question about that. But to truly set yourself and your products and services apart in the marketplace, you have to do something different than your competition, something unexpected. How you name and market your business, and how you package your products, services, and specials can help you stand out, be more memorable, and attract customers who might not otherwise show interest.

What You Call It Matters

At the start of my speaking career, I had a program called "Superior Customer Service." Clients rarely chose this program. When they did, however, they were happy with the content. I knew the speech was good, but the way I packaged it didn't attract buyers. I was complaining about this one day to a friend. She said, "Well, tell me about your speech." I replied, "I show people how hot ideas are everywhere to attract and keep new customers. You just need to know where to look for them. My speech explains this concept." She responded, "That reminds me of my favorite Mexican dish. Usually the jalapeños are mixed up in the meat sauce. I hate that. At my favorite restaurant, they make layers, and they put the jalapeños

single file across the top. I prefer it that way because I want to see the jalapeño coming. I want to know if the next bite is a hot one. Your customers are the same way. They don't want to look for the hot ideas, they want you to give them the cookbook approach to getting it done."

Later that day, I thought about what she had said: "I want to see the jalapeño coming." It was such an original phrase and it stuck in my head.

The next week, a large association called to ask if I had any topics on customer service. I'm thinking, it's a great opportunity to test-market this new phrase. So, I answered, "Yes, I have a new program titled *I Want to See the Jalapeño Coming: The Hot Recipe to Attract and Keep New Customers*." She enthusiastically replied, "This is perfect! We're doing a whole 'South of the Border' theme at our meeting!"

It was the first time a client didn't start out by asking how much I charged. We know customers buy because they're attracted to a product or service. They're not buying based on price alone, which is a good thing if something other than price is your differentiation point. Because of this name change, I had to redo some of my handouts and slides, but the work was minimal and it's still one of the most valuable 10¢ decisions I've made in my business.

I started to realize that how products and services are packaged and what they're called really matters. How does this apply to other types of industries? Let's take a peek at how some famous brands leverage clever packaging to create an advantage.

Subway used to have its famous $5 footlongs. The story of the campaign traces back to 2004, when Stuart Frankel, an owner of two Subway franchises in Miami, Florida, began selling subs for $5 on weekends and saw his sales spike without even marketing. Soon, it rippled out to other franchises and eventually became a fresh campaign for the entire brand. Add a catchy jingle, and you've got yourself a hit. They packaged it creatively, and it was a success. (Be honest, you're humming the song right now in your head, aren't you?)

Packaging That Gets Noticed

The eyewear industry offers another angle. In 1983, a man named E. Dean Butler founded LensCrafters. A couple things were happening in the industry then that made it the perfect time to start this kind of eyewear business. The biggest change was that a law had been passed that optometrists had to give patients their eyeglass prescription if they asked. Butler seized the opportunity to put stores in malls and package the service as "glasses in about an hour," knowing people would shop while they waited.

Although this fantastic idea had a definite downside in the optometric community, the concept revolutionized the eyewear industry. In a 1986 interview with *Forbes* magazine, Butler claimed, "Marketing eyewear isn't much different from selling coffee. Retailing is what you do when customers walk into a store; but with a new idea, marketing comes first. Marketing is how you inspire customers to come to your door."

How do you inspire people to come to your door? You don't have to be a famous brand to use the creative packaging concept. If you're a small company, think in terms of "10¢" short-term promotions instead of full-scale rebranding or expensive ad campaigns. I know of an oil-change business that displays a flashing sign when there's no wait. Another example is a car wash that picks a first name daily and puts it on their marquee. If it's your name and you can prove it, you get a free car wash. I have no doubt that everyone looks at the sign every time they drive by just to see if their name appears. Creative packaging like this sells because it sets you apart from the competition.

> " You don't have to be a famous brand to use the creative packaging concept. "

How You Package It Matters

As I mentioned in the prologue, I'm picky about bottled water. I can even list the top 10 bottled waters in the United States based purely on my own palate and opinion. And in fact, the entire principle of my book is based on the fact that an action doesn't have to cost a lot to make the big impact. A 10¢ decision can be as simple as

chilling a bottle of water and providing it for free. However, there is an opposite approach to packaging that is equally important. Increasing the perceived value of the product or service by investing more in the packaging also can create distinction.

For example, there was the best water experience of my life, August 25, 2009. Yes, I remember the day. My husband and I were having a romantic rendezvous in Chicago. By "romantic" I mean Cubs shirts and bleacher seats at Wrigley Field. We checked into a gorgeously decorated room. I spotted a tall table in the corner and, sitting under a spotlight, nestled in a bucket of ice, was the most beautiful bottle of water I have ever seen: frosted glass, sealed with a cork, with the word "BLING" written on the side in tiny Swarovski crystals. I swear I heard angels singing. They had bedazzled my bottle! It was truly the most breathtaking bottle I had ever seen. Two long-stem wine glasses were nearby next to an engraved sign that read "We appreciate you. Please enjoy. Additional bottles may be purchased in the gift shop for $25."

Twenty-five dollars. Really? Wow. How good must this water be?

Here's the dilemma. Do I unwrap this bad boy and see what it's like? Or do I take it home and let it live on my shelf forever as symbol of all I believe to be true about customer service?

Take a moment right now and guess. Did I open it or leave it sealed forever? Go ahead, I'll wait.

Here's what happened. I didn't crack it...I forgot to take it home!

I was devastated. It was like leaving one of my children at a rest stop! Eight years later, and I can't remember whether the Cubs won or lost or what we had for dinner. But I still remember that $25 bottle of water. What would it have tasted like? A spring fountain? A glacier?

For years afterward, I would go on and on about this from the stage, sharing the details of my never-ending wonder about this simple bottle of water. Then one day, I was speaking at a dental conference when my client came up me, after hearing this water story, and said,

Packaging That Gets Noticed

"Hey, Laurie, if you're so curious about the water, why don't you just order a bottle and find out?" (Huh…never really thought of that.)

Of course! I can end the dilemma right now. I jumped online and I found out the water now costs $49 a bottle! Talk about turning water into wine! Forget that! For $49, I can get two haircuts and a pair of pumps. (Obviously, my taste in hair and shoes doesn't match my taste in water.)

But, to my surprise, a week later, I received a box from that same client, and inside was my very own bottle of BLING water. Seriously, this bottle was so precious to me that I chilled it and saved it for New Year's Eve. A minute before midnight, I carefully unwrapped the bottle. I knew this moment would change my life.

It was finally time to taste it. I awarded them an A+ for packaging. The water inside was fine. It didn't knock my favorites off the pedestal, but the packaging made all the difference. I've even sent these as gifts many times after a speech because the impact of the bottle is so amazing. I would never consider sending a regular plastic bottle of water as a gift, even if the product inside was better. The package is what matters.

So why am I telling you all this? Why am I still talking about this bottle of water almost a decade later?

Short answer: To make a big impact, you need a little "bling." True, this water company's bling wasn't cheap. But *your* bling doesn't have to blow your budget to blow away your customers. Consider these "10¢" bits of bling.

We had a restaurant near us that was once Al Capone's Hideaway, and in between the salad and entrée courses the server would bring a palate-cleansing course. It was the tiniest dollop of lime sorbet I have ever seen on top of a tiny, pointy-ended ice cream cone, and it looked more like a pretend treat for a doll than actual adult food. But you could see grown men smiling with delight when this little bit of "bling" chased their Caesar salad.

The Gaylord Opryland Resort in Nashville has a wake-up call system with recordings of famous country music stars to wake you up with a musical greeting. I couldn't decide between Blake Shelton and Brad Paisley, so I had two calls come in an hour apart just so I could hear the creative greetings. It was a "bling" start to my day, that's for sure. Of course, this idea likely cost more than a dime. But when spread out over the number of guests who stay there annually and go home talking about this fun twist to a wake-up call that only works in Nashville, the investment is still relatively low.

Now some of you are thinking, "Our business doesn't allow for that type of creativity. There are too many regulations, or our customers won't respond to cutesy names or clever packages." Fair enough. It doesn't apply to all businesses. But do you know what does? Sincere appreciation to those who do buy your product or service. Wrapping a purchase up in sincere appreciation is a version of creative packaging that's available to every single business. And here is the best part: You can decide what level of investment you want to make in your appreciation packaging—including a free version!

When Did Saying 'Thank You' Become Hard Work?
Thank you.

Somewhere along the line, these two easy words have become hard for people to say. I don't mean the robotic phrase used at the end of a transaction: "Thank you. Have a nice day." I mean the sincere appreciation that should follow every contract signed or every referral delivered. That should come after every transaction—big or small. I am surprised how rare this genuine thank-you seems to be.

During the summer of the painted pencils, my friend Joan and I tried to sell a few other crazy things. Painted rocks, used toys, and cookies are a few that I recall. Although our products didn't fly off the shelves, those endeavors did teach me a valuable lesson about appreciation. I have a strong memory of my parents insisting we show appreciation to those who bought from us. Of course, as an adult, I now realize most of those people were making "pity purchases," because we were cute and we said thanks, and that got noticed. It wasn't a formal appreciation program, but it sure worked for us.

Packaging That Gets Noticed

Is it time for your company to consider an appreciation program? Depending on what your product or service is and how you interact with your customers, you can build an appreciation program using a stairstep approach. Be sure that your team is trained on how to deliver a proper thank-you and encourage them to be sincere and totally present when showing the appreciation to your guests.

> "...you can build an appreciation program using a stairstep approach."

Level 1: A verbal thank-you at the time of the transaction. It's most often a simple sentence used repeatedly: "Thank you for shopping with us." However, it doesn't count if the greeting sounds too robotic or is tossed out at the buyer's back as the door shuts behind him.

Level 2: A written thank-you. Though not time-consuming, it has a similar sentiment each time. Email counts, but a handwritten note sent by mail is better. This makes sense with professional services more than it does with retail, but I've seen amazing exceptions to that rule. Handwritten notes have gone by the wayside in personal and professional relationships, but it's astonishing how meaningful they can be to someone.

Level 3: The appreciation phone call. This is more content-specific to the person you're calling. Pick up that phone and thank the referral source every time you obtain a new customer who can be traced back to a specific person.

Level 4: A token gift. Although it requires an investment, a universal gift works fine. Many companies have a standard item they give to new guests. However, ask yourself if your customer really has a use for a paperweight with your company's logo on it. The money might be better spent on a coffee gift card. If you choose to send a token gift, try to find something that builds a connection with your company.

Level 5: At the top tier is a gift unique to the receiver. This requires thought, money, and time, but it can make an amazing impact. My favorite example is a referral gift I sent to an employee of a well-known company. Instead of sending a stock gift, I researched his interests. I looked on Facebook, and I found out he and his wife were big fans of an obscure band. Luckily, that band was coming to the area where he lives. So I reached out to him and said that I would love to treat him and his wife to tickets to this band's concert. He wrote back and was so surprised that I knew he liked this band and graciously accepted the offer. I bought the tickets and sent them to him with a note of thanks. Another referral followed, which was appreciation reciprocated.

No matter what your product or service is, there is room to appreciate your guests. Make sure your staff is trained to focus on a sincere thank-you at level 1. They need to add things like, "We appreciate you choosing to do business with us." If you're a business owner, you're in a position to put an appreciation campaign in place. I encourage you to have a team meeting to brainstorm ideas and then create a budget for giving thanks. Making an effort to say "thank you" has benefits you will reap for a long time to come.

There are many ways to help your business stand out from the competition, from interesting branding or unique names for your products to the "thank-you" bow you use to wrap up every guest interaction. Get creative with the big and small things that you and your staff do for your customers every day.

Packaging That Gets Noticed

Discussion Questions

How can you package your products, services, and specials to set your company apart in the marketplace?

What does your competition do that gets more attention?

What's your bling, the small "10¢" things you do that have customers talking?

In what specific ways do you and your team currently show appreciation for your guests?

Do you have a tiered thank-you program? If not, is that something to consider?

Make Progress on Your Process:
Review Your Systems for Better Service and Increased Profitability

Careful monitoring of your internal processes and systems can lead to amazing adjustments that will impact service levels or even increase profitability. Over the years, when I have explored process improvements with businesses leaders, we've often uncovered small changes that were overdue. *If that is true for you too, why haven't the small changes been made? Have you delayed making a change because of time or resistance to the idea?* In most cases, I find that either no one on the team had spotted a solution or, if they had, they didn't feel comfortable bringing it up to the boss. In other words, their attitude was Let's just keep doing what we've always done instead of really digging into the process and looking for micro-improvements. Making time to review your processes and systems is critical to long-term success.

The Catalog Creator
Soon after the painted-pencil fiasco, I was able to dust myself off and try another revolutionary idea for a young person. I invented a gift catalog. Now, you may be wondering how a child creates her own catalog, right? Well, the idea was genius, if I do say so myself. I took the most popular gift catalog of that era, *Miles Kimball*, and scoured every page looking for all the unique and fun gift items kids would love. After selecting my top 50 favorites, like the Magic 8-Ball and keychain Etch A Sketch, I carefully cut out the picture and description of the item and then clipped off the bottom right corner where the price appeared. Then I glued the square in a spiral notebook, and next to each item I raised the cost by $1 and wrote the new price in

the corner with a very fine red marker. I decorated the cover to give it my own "Laurie brand" (purple, glitter, and stickers, of course) and then confidently carried it to school to begin my sales.

This endeavor was exhilarating to me! I was a first-time business owner with every decision within my control. There was no friend pushing back on my ideas or taking half the profit. No parent telling me where to set up shop or how to price my items. My parents didn't even know I was doing this. That made it even more fun! Freedom!

Some good and some bad things came from this project. The good part is that I was the first to do anything like it in our school, so I instantly got positive attention and swarms of kids who were interested. My catalog was a top-of-the-line creation and worthy of being envied by all who wished they had a catalog business like mine. (At least that is how I remember it.) Just three days into the business, I had more cash flying around than I knew what to do with, and it was way better than selling sweet corn in the hot sun. I started to wonder how one goes about buying a cash register, because it just seemed like the next step in my company growth. I don't write that to be funny; I'm very serious. I tried to figure out where I could go to buy a cash register and how much it would weigh. Could I carry it back and forth to school? Would kids mess with it when I wasn't looking? Did it have a key so I could secure my cash drawer when I went out for recess?

Looking back, I find it interesting that I didn't consider this strange behavior, and I don't think I worried what the other kids would think of me. I truly believe in my juvenile mind I thought they would want to work for me and would be jealous that they hadn't thought of the idea themselves. This is the same feeling I get as an adult when a creative idea hits me that no one else appears to be doing.

Then came the bad stuff.

When I was ready to place my first order, I read the fine print for the first time that said I was not to send cash in the mail. How was I going to place an order by charge or check without consulting my

mother? Second, I didn't take into account what would happen when Lynette's mom called my house asking my folks why she needed to bring $20 to school for me.

Busted.

I was out of business before the first order was placed. However, when my mom sat me down to explain why I couldn't continue doing this project, she surprised me by saying we would go ahead and place the order for the things kids had already purchased. That way I could fulfill my obligations without having to embarrass myself by giving all the money back. What a great silver lining. I was so excited that I was still going to make money on this idea even though it would only be one round of sales. Oh, how short-lived that excitement was when my third lesson was about these little things called tax, shipping, and handling fees. Just like that, my entire profit was eaten up with those nasty fees that I didn't understand. What is tax and what goes into "handling" my items? Bummer. And who is this Uncle Sam guy and why did my dad say I had to pay him? Why didn't I know about all of this in advance? The answer is simple: I had not sought out help from knowledgeable advisors on running the numbers or looking at my processes.

What I learned from this business venture is that the cash that's coming in doesn't fully represent the success of the business, and my processes were extremely flawed. Being nice to your customers and providing great service is important. However, the right processes have to be in place as well. What's great about process improvement is that it only requires small changes. not an overwhelming overhaul. That means you can see great results by simply taking the time to evaluate your processes and making a few 10¢ decisions. The second thing I learned is that what I saw as freedom—running a business with no advisors—was actually the core of my downfall. I didn't know what I didn't know. If I had recognized the great advisors my parents were or even sought guidance from my much older brother, I might still be in the catalog business today!

Process Review, Are You Overdue?

I regularly conduct an activity in my workshops that leads to a group discussion on internal processes. The exercise puts a magnifying glass on the processes within an organization that are ready for change, or even elimination. I continue to be amazed by the great ideas that groups have uncovered when they dig into why certain rules, processes, and policies were originally put into place. Like the bank that estimated it was spending well over $5,000 a year generating reports for management that hadn't been looked at in years! And on top of that, the packets created by each branch were sent overnight by FedEx on a monthly basis. Once the packets arrive at the main office, the executive assistant places them on the CEO's desk. When the stack gets too big, she moves them to the floor. I asked her to indicate how high the pile was at that very moment, and she gestured about waist high. On impulse, I turned to the CEO and asked him if he remembered the last had time he actually reviewed the contents of those priority envelopes. He thought, smiled sheepishly, bowed his head an inch, and shaking it slightly from right to left, proclaimed, "Effective immediately, we will stop the report printing and mailing." Spontaneous applause erupted from the 200 staff members in attendance, and whoops were heard from those who had the responsibility of generating that work on a monthly basis. BAM! Mid-four-figure savings with just one small, smart 10¢ decision.

I call my activity the "blue towel exercise." I got the idea from a close friend who was a labor and delivery nurse at a community hospital. The hospital staff was asked to look for antiquated tasks, rules that could be challenged, wasted labor hours, or duplication of effort. One day while on shift, she noticed a laundry cart arrive on the unit with clean blue towels. These types of towels are very common in hospital systems for repeated non-sterile use. She knew what would happen to the towels next, as it was a task she had done herself many times, so this time she started a timer. The nurse on duty began the daily task of removing one towel from the laundry cart and refolding it a number of times until it was in a small square. Then she placed

the newly folded towel in a pile to her left, eventually moving the stack to a shelving unit near the delivery rooms. In the middle of this process, a circulating nurse in need of several towels grabbed the corner of one towel in each hand, shook them out flat and returned to the delivery. My friend realized immediately that the task of refolding the towels provided no value to the patient or the team. It was a labor cost they were encountering needlessly. It was obvious that eliminating that chore from their daily task list would save the hospital money.

Now, it's important to note that if you want to win someone to your way of thinking when it comes to change, it is vital that you talk in terms of *fact, not feeling.* If my nurse friend had said to the powers that be, "I think we can save some money if we quit refolding the towels," it would present as a thinking/feeling statement and be less likely to gain traction. However, if she talked in terms of facts and quantified the benefit of the change, her suggestion would be more likely to spur action.

Her recommendation was to substitute the "refolding of the towel process" with the "pivot maneuver." This, quite simply, was the act of scooping up a pile of the towels straight from the laundry cart, pivoting on the left foot, and placing them on the shelf, repeating that move until the laundry cart was empty.

Here are the facts that she presented to the management team:

Current estimated cost of refolding the towels:
- 20 minutes of labor x 3 loads a day = 1 hour of labor
- 1 hour x 260 days of deliveries x $40 (average hourly rate of nurses in department) = $10,400

Estimated cost savings of implementing the pivot maneuver:
- 1 minute of labor x 3 loads a day = 3 minutes
- 3 minutes x $1.98 (prorated salary) x 260 days = $514.80
- Savings: $9,885.20

It's obvious that eliminating this task was the way to go. But wait! My friend was asked to trace back in time where this idea originated. Figuring out why it started in the first place might help shed light on the reasoning behind the task. This is a very valuable step to include when you identify a "blue towel" in your system. Each step in a process is like a domino in a lineup. Tweak just one, or remove it altogether, and the rest of the dominos will not fall the same way. You can't remove a step in a process without fully investigating how it impacts the rest of the team downstream. In this case, I can't imagine what difference it would make, but in many of the processes I have helped review over the years, we have, on occasion, found a very solid reason why the step existed. Based on its origin, we ascertained that it would be a detriment for the system if it were eliminated without more discussion with other departments.

In the case of the blue towels at this hospital, they were able to track down a nurse who had been with the system for more than 30 years. When asked if she had any idea why everyone was trained to refold the towels this way, she was stumped. She said they had been doing it that way for as long as she could remember. Then, after a little further reflection, she replied, "Funny, now that I think about it, that's how I fold my hand towels at home."

I'm surmising by this investigative work that one day over three decades ago, the work flow was a little slow when the laundry cart arrived. "Nurse Nancy" pulled the towels and assembled them differently, maybe to fit on the shelf better or maybe just to stay busy during her shift. Very slowly over time it became "the way we do it," and each new generation of employees was taught the process during orientation. No one questioned it. No one took the initiative to stop it. Everyone just did as they were told.

Now, the only thing left to do was incorporate the process change by explaining it to each shift. Guess what happened next? The rest of the team pushed back on the change. They said things like, "That's not how we've ever done it" or "I don't think that's going to work." Because of the pushback and lack of compliance, the process was

never changed! My friend doesn't work at that hospital anymore, but the last time she checked, the towels were still refolded daily, costing this hospital hundreds of thousands of dollars in the 10 years since I first heard this story.

Is the Change Worth the Challenge?

Recently, a nurse attending a program where I shared the blue towel exercise approached me afterward with a perfect example of how questioning an internal policy that doesn't make sense can lead to a surprising discovery. She explained that in the mid-1970s she worked in a 12-step recovery center where all of the shifts began on the 5's, meaning her start time was 8:05 a.m. After working there a few months, she began to wonder why the start time wasn't at the traditional top of the hour, so she asked her supervisor, who had no idea. "It's just always been that way," was her reply. She tried to dig a little deeper and repeatedly got the same answer. Apparently, no one seemed to know why this policy existed.

Like a dog with a bone, she would not let it go. Her determination to figure this out led to the suggestion that she come in early one day and talk to the nurse who has been there "forever" and was in charge of that department years ago. She expressed her frustration that no one knew the answer and never thought to challenge it. The nurse she was talking to burst out laughing and said to her, "Oh, I know why. Do you remember the TV show M*A*S*H?" She replied, "Of course I do. I'm a nurse. We all watched it." The veteran nurse continued, "Well, it showed on Thursday nights and ended at 10:30 p.m. I wanted to watch it, so I changed bed checks to 10:35 p.m. so I could see the end of the episodes. So, it was just easier to have all the shift changes match up. Shift change occurred 30 minutes after bed checks, or 11:05 p.m. This makes the morning shift begin at 8:05 a.m. Ta-da! Your start time!"

It turns out that because it was a 12-step recovery center, it was important that the residents' daily experience be very routine: Get up at the same time, eat at the same time, go to bed at the same time. Hence, the bed check needed to be the same every night.

But long after the show was off the air and the M*A*S*H fan had moved on to a new position, the starting times remained the same. I asked the nurse who told me this story if they changed it after this conversation. She laughed, "Nope! Stayed that way the rest of my days at that job!"

In this case, the anomaly didn't impact the center's process or profitability, so I can see why they didn't upset the system or the residents by changing it after years of the same routine. However, it's a perfect example of a policy that is put in place—and stays in place—for a reason that has nothing to do with the customer. Sound familiar?

A great example of a success story when it comes to change in policy occurred when an administrator of a surgery center launched a "cost-cutting campaign." Every staff person was asked to try to come up with one thing that could be done to decrease cost or increase revenue. The supply manager made the recommendation to change the type of paper towels used throughout the clinic. For years, the center had used a C-fold towel. The downside of the design of this product is that a majority of the time, multiple paper towels came out of the dispenser, causing waste. The manager said that by changing to a Z-fold design, each towel would come out of the dispenser as a single sheet. The best news is that she could get the product from the same vendor for the same price. All she had to do was change the code number of the item ordered, and get nine doctors to agree to the change. She accomplished this task and estimated the savings at roughly $1,600 a year. The cost to the clinic to make this change was zero. While you might read this and think that doesn't sound like a lot of money, keep in mind it was just one of many ideas implemented at the same time that, when pooled together, made a significant difference. Small changes paid off big.

Making Change Happen

Getting people involved who are impacted by the adjustments is the most effective way to implement change. Gather your team and present the situation in a premise that I like to call "blame the convention." Most managers attend at least one association meeting, continuing-education event, or convention per year. Upon their return, many new ideas and suggestions are foisted upon unsuspecting staff. It's not uncommon for the staff to have little to no control over the changes and, therefore, every reason to put up barriers to a smooth change in procedures.

> Getting people involved is the most effective way to implement change.

As a manager, instead consider presenting the situation that needs review and bringing the team into the discussion. Hash through *what* can be changed, *why* the change would help, and *how* it could be implemented. Start by saying something like, "When I was at the conference, an idea was brought up in one of the sessions about looking at processes, antiquated rules, and steps we might be doing because it's the way we have always done it. The speaker challenged us to bring our teams together and ask for help to identify our issues and see what adjustments we can make. We want the solutions to help reduce cost, increase profit, or improve our service levels internally and externally."

Afterward, open up the floor to discussion with the team; or, if you have a workforce too large for one discussion, divide them into tables of five to seven people and give them a block of time to come up with processes that fit the criteria of change that you proposed. You may be surprised how often the team will present the exact same situation that you were going to suggest. Here is the best part: This approach gives you the opportunity to give credit to others for creating and implementing the idea, which will lead to faster results with less pushback.

In the clinic where I worked for almost 18 years, we facilitated lively group discussions at a management level by executing a problem-solving grid. The initial idea for the grid—and the first four questions—came from a concept in Dale Carnegie's book *How to Stop Worrying and Start Living*. From there, we evolved it over the years and added questions to meet our needs. Here's how it works.

The following questions were analyzed, with the final answers placed in a grid. It allowed for an impartial discussion and consistent follow-up on assigned tasks.

- What is the specific problem?
- What causes are contributing to the problem?
- What are some possible solutions to the problem?
- Which solution will best solve the problem?
- To whom is the solution delegated? (Could be an individual or a group, but names must be listed.)
- What are the steps to completion? (A broad overview is acceptable.)
- What is the deadline for the next step?
- What is the deadline for the entire change to take place?
- What is the cost?
- What is the desired outcome?

The key to process review as an owner or a management-level team member is to be open-minded. Innovative ideas start with asking questions differently and being willing to change the old ways of doing things in order to grow and thrive.

Discussion Questions

When was the last time you reviewed your processes and systems?

What are the "blue towels" in your organization?

How might you sell the idea of change to your organization?

What roadblocks do you anticipate when making a change?

Is a cost-cutting idea challenge a good idea for your company at this time?

Service from the Inside Out:
It Pays to Focus on Internal Customer Service

Only paying attention to the needs of your external customer will result in an unbalanced triad between the manager, staff, and customer. *Have you spent time creating a communication plan for your internal customer? Does your team have a training module dedicated to mutual respect inside the workplace?* A cohesive, balanced team is found when the needs of the staff and leaders are taken into consideration as much as the needs of the customer.

The Value of Authentic Appreciation

My career in the chiropractic world ended abruptly on a Friday afternoon in January when I was 21 solely because I felt undervalued and underappreciated. When I look back on that experience, I realize that may not have been a true assessment of the situation. However, it's sure how I felt at the time. I probably needed a little maturity to better understand and respond to those feelings. Regardless, I left a field in which I received an expensive education, had a good job and several years of experience in my pocket, and had an opportunity to grow within that practice. This story is a little embarrassing to retell because, in hindsight, I can see what a small issue it was that triggered my departure. But I didn't think it was little deal at the time. Here's what happened.

At the end of each day, the doctor would stand at the end of a long hallway, give us a wave, and say "Thanks a lot!" Then out the door he would go. It was a blanket statement just tossed our way without meaning or direction to any one team member. In fact, it was so robotic and unspecific that once in a while when we heard his keys jangling in his office door, which signified his imminent departure

followed immediately by the repeatable phrase, my co-worker would whisper to me in a voice to imitate him, "Thanks a lot." We would both giggle immaturely when, two seconds later, he would bellow the three words and then leave.

Fast-forward to a Friday in the fall of 1985. We had 100 patients to see that day. I was the only staff member who could take X-rays and do some of the other clinical tasks. Right before lunch, he did something that I did not care for, and, being young and immature, I decided that it was as good a day as any to quit, without notice! I thought to myself, "If he isn't going to appreciate the work I am doing, then he can find someone else. I don't need to put up with this."

Looking back, I hang my head in shame that I didn't slow my roll and calm down a little bit before taking such a hasty action. Instead, I wrote him a scathing two-page letter about his lack of appreciation and left it lying on his desk with my key. I squealed out of the parking lot, leaving him high and dry with an entire afternoon of patients to see without my help. Wow, it pains me to write this story, but I must. Why? Because the lesson is so valuable.

Fifteen years go by, and I have not been back to the office or run into the doctor around town. I suffer from migraine headaches, and he was the only one who had been able to eliminate them from my life through cervical adjustments. I tried other chiropractors after I left his employment, but no one was getting it done for me like he did. One day in the middle of a terrible episode, I got the bright idea that I could make an appointment to return as if I were a new patient. I was married now, so my last name was different; I didn't look the same; and he had so much turnover in staff I thought he wouldn't even remember me. I would pay cash and therefore not even have to give my Social Security number or insurance information. Why I thought this would work I have no idea; it must have been the headache clouding my judgment.

I called for an appointment, and they agreed to get me in the same day since I was in pain. While waiting for him to appear in the exam room, my heart started to pound as I realized what a stupid idea this was. What if he recognized me as the woman who left him high and dry at lunchtime more than a decade and half before? I heard his steps coming down the hall and I thought to myself: Abort mission,

abort mission! He opened the door, and as soon as we made eye contact there was instant recognition. He glanced down at my chart, glanced back up, hand on hip, smiled and said, "Well, Laurie, that's a pretty long lunch hour you just took, don't you think?" We both started laughing and then I profusely apologized for my incredibly unprofessional behavior all those years before. He was so gracious about it and then he said, "Laurie, can I ask you a question? In your letter to me, which I still have in my files, you talked about how I never showed any appreciation. Didn't I say 'thank you' every single day?"

That's when I realized that he had no idea he wasn't connecting with his silent signals or his verbal ones. At the time, I just made light of the situation and decided not to get into a whole discussion about my real reasons for leaving and the fact that it went deeper than the letter could explain. But I realized as he talked that he was very sincere in his confusion over my abrupt parting.

By this time, I was presenting professional-development programs to healthcare providers and started to pay attention to the fact that many didn't know how to properly praise their employees. They needed an easy-to-remember "phrase of praise" so it could be automatic yet heartfelt. To help that situation I came up with a very simple three-step appreciation formula.

Build a Three-Layer 'Thanks Cake'

Think of praise like frosting on a cake. You want it evenly spread, not too thick in any one spot. To spread the praise just right, my formula has three easy steps. It's the person's *name,* followed by *what* you're praising them for, and ending with *why* it makes a difference. And, be sure you're looking them in the eye as you say it.

Imagine hearing someone say, "Hey everybody, good job today."

That's just white noise, a blanket praise.

Now, listen to the difference using the formula: "Betty, the way you handled that angry customer today was fantastic. By the time we met with her, she had calmed down, and things went much, much better. Thank you."

Hear the difference?

- "Betty"—use the person's name
- "the way you handled that angry guest today was fantastic"—identify what you're praising them for
- By the time we met with her, she had calmed down, and things went much, much better."—tell them why it made a difference

Though it sounds a little odd and rehearsed, in real life with the sincerity of the situation, it is a huge improvement over "Thanks a lot" or "Great job today." Simple, right? Worth the "10¢" change in thinking? You bet. Get out there and praise someone today. Sincere praise is the gasoline between paychecks and one of the easiest staff-development tools that I offer.

Treating Staff with Respect

Many times people leave a job because they feel underappreciated by co-workers or leadership. So it's logical that we can retain more staff if both bosses and co-workers learn to be more appreciative of the people around them.

Paying attention to internal customer service is as vital as your external efforts. For several years, I did consulting work with small businesses to help them create a solid foundation of service using all of the tools shared in this book. What I found over time was a commonality among those who struggled. They were weak in their efforts when it came to internal customer service. Where were they lacking? They didn't treat their staff with respect, teammates weren't truly working together for the greater good of the organization, and they didn't show a commitment to lifelong learning for improvement on personal communication skills. The more I dug into backstories or the history of past grievances, the more layers of crud I would find.

I once joked with a client that being a consultant who problem-solves is like peeling back scabs and suctioning the pus out of the old sores. Yes, too graphic of a description, I know. But it's accurate. Many times managers would tell me it was better to just leave the healed "scab" alone and work around the issue rather than opening up old wounds. That's one perspective. I believe that an even better

idea is to put expectations in place that decrease the chance of "injury" happening by finding ways to prevent the problem in the first place.

Leading with the Heart of a Parent

As the boss, owner, executive director, administrator, manager, or anyone with a role leading others, your job is to keep staff "between the ditches." For any of you who have raised a child, when he or she turned 16 I am confident that many of you had a conversation with your teen driver that sounded something like this: "Sweetheart, if you ever find yourself at a party where you don't belong and you have had too much to drink, please call me at any hour of the night and I will come and get you, no questions asked." Sound familiar? The reason so many of us have had this discussion is because our job as parents is to keep the kid between the ditches, preferably on their side of the middle line. We spend years guiding and coaching them to make good decisions, and when they begin to stray, just like when driving a car, we hear the rumble strips on the side of the road that warn of impending danger. If the driver reacts immediately, it really isn't a big deal. Steer back onto the road and continue rolling along. But if the rumble-strip noise is ignored or they go over it too fast for it to matter, the next stop could be upside-down in the ditch. Hopefully, with a little help from a tow truck and support from others, we can get them right side up without a lot of permanent damage. But when it goes sideways in big ways, there can be life-changing moments or even fatal results. It's a dark metaphor, but spot-on.

> **Leading staff with the heart of a parent changes how one manages.**

Leading staff with the heart of a parent changes how one manages. Constantly advising and guiding people back onto the accepted track is critical. What that means in office life is that you must educate the staff on expected behaviors, give verbal affirmations when things are going well, and provide very timely redirects when needed. It is a huge mistake to let the errors build up in a pile to be shared all at once at an annual review. See "teachable moments" as the rumble strips and use them often. The

best approach is to be professional, courteous, and encouraging, rather than making staff members feel like they are in trouble. In the same manner that a kid can go to a trusted parent to confide in when things are going off-track, creating that same level of trust between management and staff is imperative.

'10¢' Tools to Improve Consistency and Productivity of Your Team

Internal customer-service and respect issues can flare up when everyone isn't working toward the same goal or if some people aren't pulling their weight. Do lack of consistency and low productivity impact your work environment? Here are three specific small-change techniques that can help.

1. Hold weekly one-on-one meetings with a notebook in hand

Hallway management can get you in trouble fast. You're walking down the hall, you see someone you manage, and you stop them with an instruction. They listen, nod, and then you both continue on your way. With no formal interaction, with no chance for the employee to document the new information, and with no paper trail to prove you even informed him or her of the information, it is likely that the instruction is lost. Also, with this type of management, the only time employees get an audience with you is when they knock first.

Instead, consider quick, formal, one-on-one meetings on a regular basis. I know this sounds simple, but it's amazing how many people I've met who don't have an opportunity to meet with a boss or co-workers on a regular basis. I chose once a week for the team I was managing. Of course, for you it may need to be more or less frequent. The point is, the employee needs to come with a notebook or an electronic device for documentation. The bullet points of the meeting should be written down, decisions made, dates and deadlines added, and then both people need to sign off on this document when the meeting is over. It's nothing fancy, but it's consistent. It was amazing how often I thought I'd been clear, and in reviewing our meeting notes, I found out I wasn't understood properly.

2. Figure out your MBAs, also known as "making-bank activities"

We all have activities we do during the course of a day that make us feel productive but likely don't lead to increased revenue or decreased expense, which are the two things that lead to profit.

I used to make a list of all the things I'd already done during the day just so I could use my trusty highlighter to cross them off. Although it was a colossal waste of time, it sure made me feel a sense of accomplishment. But it wasn't an activity that helped me "make bank." Make a list of your daily activities that provide the best results to meet your goals. Put them in priority order and then be consistent in attending to those things first.

If you have support staff who will handle some of these things for you, you have time to concentrate on other things. Evaluate whether those other things that you're doing are a good use of your time and whether they make you more productive.

I was once hired by a doctor to watch him during patient hours because he wanted to learn why he was always running behind. He wanted to know how to change his systems and processes to make him and his team more productive. My observation revealed that between every patient, he would leave the floor, go back to his office, and check his email or maybe make a personal phone call. He didn't like it when I told him that there didn't appear to be anything wrong with his *systems* or the work ethic of his staff. It was his choice of activities during patient hours that was wreaking havoc with his schedule. He fired me before the end of the day, but my feedback was accurate. My untimely termination was a clear signal that he wasn't planning to change his behavior. He wanted his systems to be the problem, when it was actually the "making-bank activities" that were causing his productivity problems.

3. Adopt a one-pass system.

Our office had a one-pass philosophy that impacted his level of success. That means he would touch a file one time, complete everything that was necessary, and then pass it along to the next staff person who needed the file. He would not allow a stack of charts to sit in a pile, waiting on answers to questions. He felt that

a lot of time was wasted shuffling papers around. I bought into the same philosophy in my office. When I'm self-disciplined enough to follow my own rules, it makes a huge difference. When the task comes in, take action on it immediately all the way to completion whenever possible. That means all the way to the cabinet and its proper resting folder. How I wish I would listen to myself on this all the time. Piles, piles, and more piles surround me in my office and in my home.

Despite my lack of discipline, I know that this secret awesome sauce is available to me. All I have to do is use it, and now you can too. Touch it once. Finish, file, and put it to rest. If it needs further action, then properly document, set a reminder in a tracking system that works for you, and then store it where you can find it until the earliest possible time that you can resolve the task. It works like a dream, even if you are not paper-based and everything is electronic.

For more consistency and increased productivity in your workplace, initiate frequent, formal one-on-one meetings, concentrate on activities that lead to increased revenue and decreased expense, and adopt a one-pass system to complete tasks.

Take Advantage of Teachable Moments

After several years as a department manager in the clinic where I worked, we decided to attempt 360-degree evaluations. This process, also known as multi-rater feedback, was first started in the 1950s and gained popularity in the mid-1990s. The concept is that assessments are not only done by your superior, but also include input from your subordinates and colleagues, as well as a self-evaluation.

We were asked that during our staff evaluations we pose this important question: "What can I do that would help make your job go more smoothly?" No problem, I thought. I could ask, but I felt very confident that I was very in tune with what my staff of 15 needed and wanted from me as their leader. There shouldn't be any surprises.

The first employee review I conducted after this task was assigned was with my transportation manager. Her job was to make sure that all patients needing a ride to our clinic were assigned to one of the cars in our fleet and that drivers were scheduled to make the

appropriate runs. Joyce did an excellent job for me and rarely needed any close supervision. She was organized, trustworthy, and a very hard worker. I knew this evaluation would go without a single hitch, done in 10 minutes max. When we got to the end of my report out to her, I closed by explaining to her that we were trying something new this year with the 360-degree evaluations, and as part of that process, I was to ask her this magic question for direct feedback.

I totally expected her to say she had nothing for me. That's not to say I thought I was a perfect boss. I just made the assumption that if something were wrong with my internal service, my staff would be direct enough to let me know right when it happened. An internal "rumble strip," if you will. But instead of just giving me a thumbs-up, she said, "Yes, actually there is something you can do for me. When we have our weekly meetings, you go through your agenda really fast and then you get up and walk out before I even have a chance to go over things on my list. I could do my job better if before you leave, you asked if I had anything I needed to cover." I remember feeling very defensive immediately to this feedback. Unfortunately, one of my personality flaws is that I am a really fast talker. It's not fast in my head, but it is to those who have to communicate with me. Joyce happens to be a slow talker, and that means that too often I would cut her off or finish her sentences without even realizing it. Not letting people have a chance to share what they are thinking is poor management, and I am not alone in that leadership mistake.

> Not letting people have a chance to share what they are thinking is poor management...

By being open to this incoming teachable moment, I was able to work on this skill. Each time I met with her after that, I tried to remember what she needed from me. It is an offer that costs absolutely nothing, yet the benefit was significant.

The Secret to Retaining Good Staff

Following are three common-sense ideas, often overlooked by employers, for retaining good people and building long-term professional relationships.

1. Provide continuing education on a regular basis

Make it a top priority to send your staff to educational programs in your industry. Encourage your team to become members of any state or local organizations that are pertinent to your product or service. If there is no such thing, then create "on-site" teaching moments. Employees who feel they are growing in their position—and who see that you are invested in that growth—will stay longer. You would never think of denying your children a chance to go to school, yet many staff people are denied "work schooling" that could make a big difference to their careers.

2. Build opportunities for growth

Plan annual retreats and develop long-term action plans. Focus on personal growth for each team member along with your larger business goals. Allow shadowing of different areas of the company so overall knowledge is as widespread as possible. On occasion, send key staff people to visit others in your industry in a non-compete area so they can bring back business-building ideas to share with the team.

3. Acknowledge productivity. Increased customer volume directly benefits a business owner

The staff, on the other hand, may only see growth as more work. Recognize hard work with an individualized reward system that increases morale. The key to this idea is to determine what each staff member feels a good "reward" would be. Doughnuts for breakfast may not always be the extra-special treat you anticipated. While one person would like a small cash bonus, a working parent might appreciate time off to catch his or her child's soccer game on a Thursday afternoon. If bonus options are not possible in your organization, then at the very least consider using sincere praise and appreciation.

In summary, if you want to know how to find and keep good people, think of it like any other great relationship. Find staff people who have similar interests and values, then treat them like treasured family members. Open communication, mutual respect, time for fun, and plans for a future together will build a long-term professional relationship.

Discussion Questions

Is there a healthy dose of praise going around in your organization? Are you giving as well as receiving?

What can be done to increase the consistency and productivity of your team? Be specific.

What can be done to increase your consistency and productivity? Be specific.

Which of the secrets to retraining good staff are areas you could improve on?

How would you rate the overall internal customer-service levels today in your organization or the department you manage?

Behaviors That Build Business:
Using a Game Mindset to Win

Building business is not easy. If it were, everyone would do it. *Do you have rules that contribute to the success of your business? Is the team aware of the philosophies leadership has when it comes to building a successful company?* In this chapter, we look at four behaviors that build business. Each is simple to understand but may not always be easy to deliver.

Monopoly Tournament Champion

Years ago, Hasbro had a nationwide Monopoly competition that led to a world champ, and at 12 years old that became my dream. I stumbled across the advertisement for the event in our newspaper. My mom had it open on the kitchen table one morning while I was eating my Cocoa Puffs. I can still see the ad in the lower-right corner: "Kane County Monopoly Tournament, Sponsored by Hornsby's Department Store." It had the image of Mr. Monopoly— you know, the guy with the top hat, cane, and thick mustache? He was beckoning me to register, so we did.

My training for this event, like any Olympic-level competitor, was vigorous. I played almost daily on a board that had great sentimental value. As far back as I can remember, on rainy afternoons my mom would get out that board and we would start a game. We'd have cheddar cheese on Ritz crackers and pop (that's soda to you East Coast people) in crystal wine glasses. The board was marbled with brown age spots and the play money was rice-paper thin from years of being passed between hands. When I removed the box lid, I could smell the wave of musty cardboard from the years of storage in our farmhouse attic.

Mom would tease me by saying she wanted to be the iron playing piece, knowing that was my first choice. We would pretend argue over who would get it, which is funny to me because today I wouldn't fight over an iron in any situation. The biggest thing I remember is that my mom never just "let me win." If I was going to get bragging rights, I would have to earn them fair and square. No cheating, and definitely no gimmes.

She was a great teacher: patient, fun, and always sprinkling life lessons in between the dice rolls. When we had to suspend play because it was getting late or it was time to cook dinner, she would say, "OK, we each get one more roll, and then we have to put it up until another day." Mom never allowed us to just quit in the middle of a game. Even to this day, I can't stand to declare an early winner by default. There is always another day to pick it up where we left off until our game is complete.

So, after I took my last turn, she would gently pick up the board at the seam, being careful to keep it from bending in half. She would slowly walk the eight and half steps from the kitchen to the dining room and slide the board onto the table without ever toppling over the houses and hotels we had built. This small action made me feel so valued and important, instead of treating me like just another task stuck into her day. I'm now a middle-aged woman and my mother has been gone almost nine years. What I wouldn't give for just one more roll.

All of that practice for the competitive Monopoly event paid off. I won in the first round and officially claimed the title of local Monopoly Tournament Champion! What a thrill it was. As an adult, I realized that the behaviors in the game of Monopoly are the same behaviors that can help you build your business. Here are the four that matter most.

Behaviors That Build Business

1. Know what people land on most frequently

Because I know that in the game of Monopoly players land on the orange properties the most, I work to grab those first. It's the same with your customers. Do you know what makes them come to your place of business? Do you know what *really* brings them back to see you repeatedly? You may think it's the chocolate-chip cookie you offer them while they wait, but it might be the fact that the first encounter person always knows their name and treats them kindly.

Is it possible that you don't even know why people choose you? Is it more of a guess on your part? Then it's time to do some research so you can discover your stats using facts, not feelings.

> **Successful businesses have reinvested in their biggest resource: the staff.**

2. Build early and build often

The sooner you can afford to build houses and put them on your Monopoly property, the more likely it is that you're going to win. There are so many ways for us to spend our resource dollars in business, but I believe the behavior that will build your business is to focus on staff needs before filling your own pockets. That may be hard for business owners to hear, but in the two decades that I've been working with clients, I've found one thing to be universally true: Successful businesses have reinvested in their biggest resource: the staff. When I say reinvest, I don't mean provide raises and benefits. I mean investing in time, education, training, personal-development opportunities, and relationships at work.

We all know how costly it is to replace staff. Learning to build early and build often by developing your people is critical.

3. Play by the rules

I think almost everyone has at least one house rule when they play Monopoly. These are tweaks to the original instructions that, when used often enough, become a part of the player's belief that the rule is real. For example, are you one of those families who puts a little money in the middle of the board, and then when you land on Free

Parking, you get the extra cash? That's not a real rule. Once you agree to play by the rules outside of the original game, then the manner in which you win changes. The same is true in business.

If you have policies for how things are supposed to be done and they exist for a good reason, then honor them from the top down. If the frontline person enforces a policy and the customer asks to speak to a manager, it's imperative that the next level of authority stand strong in the same stance as often as possible. Otherwise, the customer knows they have found a path to a different answer.

I realize a fine line exists between giving customers everything you can to make them happy and respecting the rules you have in place. I often say to managers and owners, "If you let a customer go around your staff and get a different answer from yours, be prepared to handle that customer for the rest of your days. She will never accept anything the staff tells her again if she can get a better answer from you."

4. Don't forget why you got the game board out in the first place

I love to play games, and any time I can convince friends to get out a deck of cards or open the box lid to a board game, I am giddy with anticipation of fun. One thing I can say without hesitation is I am a good loser. Even though I have a competitive spirit, I never let that get the best of me by feeling angry or frustrated when I lose. I truly just want everyone to enjoy the experience. I'd like to suggest that we remind ourselves of this in business too. Why did we get into this field in the first place? What's fun about the people who are sharing this experience with you daily? What can you let go that brings anger or frustration? What actions can you take to make your time together as fun as it can be, given your circumstances?

There you have it. Four ways to build your business with a game mindset.

The Remedy for Those Who Play Alone

One thing I love about being an entrepreneur without a large staff is the speed at which I can change things. I literally can make things happen overnight. It's true! I can go to bed one day making a decision on something I want to start doing or stop doing and the very next morning I can make it be so, like magic.

One thing I don't like about being an entrepreneur without a large staff is that all decisions rest on my shoulders. The enemy of forward movement is indecision. Because I do not have a board to report to or a team to be accountable to, it means I am totally in charge. If you are a small-business owner, you can relate to this section of the book. What do you do when there is no one to lean on, to hash it out with, or share responsibility with?

> **The enemy of forward movement is indecision.**

I found the answer in a system of camaraderie shared by a colleague many years ago: Create a personal board of directors (PBOD). This "10¢" concept is so simple, but incredibly effective. A personal board of directors is a small group of people you invite into your inner circle regarding your business. That might include a colleague in the same industry, a trusted friend with a business mind, an accountant, an attorney, a previous manager, or any other confidant who comes to mind. The team is asked to connect with you as needed—maybe all at once, as a summit of the minds, or individually over the year. Their role is to take an active part in understanding your business.

When a small group of people who do not work for you understands the challenges, opportunities, and decisions facing you on a regular basis, you have a safety net of sorts. I chose two different groups of people for my PBOD. The first is my mastermind group, which consists of five people in my niche industry of professional speaking, three men and two women. Each of us brings something special and unique to the group, and we have a level of confidentiality, concern, and support that makes a difference in my professional life. They all are very successful at what they do, and I trust them to challenge my thinking and applaud my success, all in the same call. I, in return,

provide that same level of commitment to each of them. Because we live in different parts of the country, we meet six times a year through video calls and only once a year in person. This PBOD is very important to me and helps me make swift decisions in my business.

My other PBOD is a group of local people who meet with me one-on-one. One is my financial planner, who also worked beside me at my corporate job for more than 18 years and built her business at the same time I did. My other PBOD members are an amazing graphic designer, an accountant, a social-media expert, two close friends, my niece, and my husband, Tom, who is an attorney and my business partner. Yes, some of these people are paid independent contractors, but they also play a role for me that is as important as the service they are paid to provide. I can call any one of the board members and openly talk to him about something I am contemplating or a decision I need to make but can't quite do without help. It's through deductive reasoning, challenging questions, or brilliant suggestions that I am able to move forward or get unstuck.

Whether you are solopreneur, small-business owner, or a business executive, I believe having a personal board of directors is critical to your success. Surround yourself with people who believe in your aspirations and truly want to see you succeed. People fitting that description may not be at the place where you earn your paycheck. They may be around the corner or across the world, so make time to find them and officially invite them into your PBOD.

By reaching out to circles of influence for advice, you can impact your energy to keep playing the game of work.

Discussion Questions

What are the reasons your customers keep coming back?

How are you reinvesting in your staff on a regular basis?

Does the management team back up the staff when it comes to policy enforcement?

Do you like the idea of a personal board of directors? If yes, who are your five picks to play?

Are there people currently in your inner circle who do not believe in your aspirations or truly want you to succeed? What, if anything, should you do to correct this?

Secrets to Building
a Service-Oriented Team:
Tips to Retain and
Train Great Talent

A big part of superior service starts with the ability to find and retain great talent in the workforce. *How well are you doing as a company in finding the right fit? Do you know what is motivating the next generation of adults in the workforce?* Taking the time to understand the views of others will help you learn how to fuel the fire that motivates each of your employees to provide great service.

A Light-Bulb Moment in Motivation

When our daughter, Ellie, was little, she struggled with settling into her big-girl bed for a good night's sleep. Each night for a week, she would shuffle into our room and want to sleep with us instead of alone in her room. Having been warned by many that once you capitulate to that request there is no going back, we remained firm that she must sleep in her own bed. This was met with temper tantrums and a nightly scene that caused great stress.

Looking for any solution, I turned to a book on child rearing for help. I read a suggestion to remove things one at a time until she complied. Only then would we know her true currency. We were willing to try anything. So that night at bedtime, we explained to Ellie, in language a 3-year-old could understand, that if she did not settle down as asked, we would remove her stuffed animals, and wait 15 minutes. If that didn't work, we would move on to her books, and so forth. Privately my husband had inquired, "How far

are we willing to go with this idea?" I firmly responded, "All the way. We will take everything out of this room if we have to." He agreed and we stood united.

After we asked Ellie if she understood of all of this, she nodded and laid down after her bedtime story. We left the room proud that the threat of removing her things was enough to fix our problem. That joy was short-lived. Less than three minutes later, she appeared beside me, fussing about the bed situation. So before I even had the chance to put on my nighttime face cream, we had to initiate the launch sequence. We took out the mound of stuffed animals while she watched and screamed. Fifteen minutes later she was still ramping up, so we took out all the books. This process continued for a long time until there was nothing left in the room but Ellie and the bed. I looked at my husband with complete despair that this idea had failed, and he said, "Get the screwdriver. I'll take apart the bed."

We were two hours into this nightmare and found ourselves with a room that was empty except for a sleeping bag and a crying kid with a blanket in her hand. And then it happened. I stepped into the middle of the room and raised my arms above my head to start removing the glass globe on the ceiling fan in order to take out the light bulb, since it was the only thing left to take. Ellie stopped abruptly, and in between small baby gulps of air, she said, "Whatcha doing?" I replied sternly, "I told you we would take everything out of this room until you lay down and go to sleep like a big girl." She wiped the last tear and said in a very bold voice, "OK, I'll stop." She curled up on the sleeping bag and closed her eyes. Shocked, I glanced at Tom, and without skipping a beat he said, "Wow, I really wish we would have started with the light bulb!"

We all know that it is more expensive to find and hire a new recruit than it is to develop the talent we already have on board. Taking the time to figure out what motivates them, how their communication styles differ, and what role generational differences play will have the greatest impact on retention and boost your service level.

Four Reasons for Retention Failure

Acquiring good staff is only half the battle of business. Retaining talent can be an even bigger challenge. Digging into the possible cause of retention failure is a smart place to start when analyzing your team's satisfaction. Here are four factors that affect retention and that can impact how motivated your team members are to provide the level of service you expect.

1. Ignoring generational differences in the workplace

I first heard about generational differences during the beginning stages of my leadership training in the early '90s. A fellow manager read an article about the topic and felt strongly that all of us on the leadership team needed to pay attention to generational diversity. She wanted us to understand how the era in which a team member is born impacts one's ability to communicate, connect, and lead. We were in a rapid stage of growth, hiring people faster than we could print the orientation packets! Our new hires ranged from doctors in their 50s to entry-level staff in their late teens, so we required some serious communication chops in order to keep everyone on the same page.

While it made sense to me that your birth year influences your core values, work ethic, and communication style, I thought a deep dive into the topic was kind of frivolous, a novelty theme for us to browse. Our entire management team had to read a book on it, participate in a group discussion, and attempt to implement strategy for better communication based on the content. But, to be totally honest, most of us pushed it aside, seeing it as a management fad. We didn't put it in the forefront of our daily behavior. Interestingly enough, as we experienced growing pains, we also had some retention issues. In fact, one department had a turn of more than 35 people in just over two years, and we blamed that situation on several factors, none of them being generational.

Now fast-forward more than 25 years, and I have met and become friends with experts who can prove the value of this concept to the health of an organization. I have no doubt that we could have retained many of the people we lost over the years by understanding

their generation better and working harder to meet their needs, not only the needs of our business. Clearly, we were on the cutting edge of this material years ago and I didn't grab onto it. Don't let the same thing happen to you.

In my quest over the past few years to learn as much as I could about this topic, I began to follow the work of generational expert Anna Liotta. As founder of the Generational Institute and author of *Unlocking Generational CODES*™, Anna has helped many companies, including Amazon and Microsoft, as well as the PGA and the NBA, retain top talent and loyal clients from every generation.

To dig a little deeper for this book, I interviewed Anna, asking several key questions about generational diversity. It's important to realize that the Generational CODES are not an absolute, but rather an incredible tool to help understand others in a way that helps you to deliver exceptional customer service.

While there may be some debate among experts on the specific years assigned to each group, the following range provides an accurate picture of the five generations currently present in the workforce.

- Traditionalists, born before 1946
- Baby boomers, born between 1946 and 1964
- Gen Xers, born between 1965 and 1979
- Millennials, born between 1980 and 1999
- Globals (Gen Z), born after 1999

What I learned from Anna is that people often can get defensive when they are categorized, particularly Gen Xers. One of their key codes is that they see themselves as individuals, thinking "There's no one like me." They grew up feeling like outliers and didn't want to be part of a group. So the moment you call them a group, they adamantly disagree until one starts to describe some of the isolated experiences and how they often show up in the workplace. Then, they say with a puzzled expression, "How do you know that about me? I thought I was the only one."

With all of that said, there may always be a characteristic or a personal experience that separates an individual from their larger code. What a code is really looking at is all the variables that are engaged in the process or rules that drives one's actions and reactions. Those imprints, experiences, and emotions are all little pieces of the algorithm. Then you see the outcome, called actions and reactions. But there will always be individuals who respond to it differently.

It's important for leaders to understand Generational CODES because the entire young-adult workforce, ages 21 to 40, currently consists of Millennials. They make up a larger percentage of the workforce than any other generation. Not understanding what drives them to take great care of your customers is like trying to deliver customer service with both hands tied behind your back.

One of the biggest things that impacts our service levels is the *churn and turn of talent.* And when leaders don't understand what drives their people, they are basically trying to recruit in the dark.

Often, leaders just want to find people who will respond to the same Generational CODES of service that they do. So they keep trying to find what they think are the "good" Millennials, who may be the ones whose parents raised them more like Gen Xers, and therefore are closer to the leader's way of thinking.

That strategy must change. Now we must be much more competent and be explicit about what we think good service is. We need to make it a priority to document, train, and give examples of exceptional service. It's vitally important to have training, because leaders need the specifics so we can move from *our* implicit to *their* explicit actions.

Here are Anna Liotta's three C's to consider when setting, training, and reinforcing your service expectations:

Common sense. Organizations that don't provide clear customer-service expectations are basically saying, "We're good with whatever you bring to the table." If you drop staff into a position without customer-service training, you will unknowingly create an eclectic delivery of standards. Each team member's personal customer-service experience during their formative years becomes their normal or the "common sense" they're referencing when carrying out their duties. That set of early events and experiences create an imprint, or Generational CODES.

> **Because we think that good customer service has an element of common sense, we get bamboozled by our own blind spots.**
> —Anna Liotta

Anna believes that good customer service has an element of common sense, we get bamboozled by our own blind spots.

Here's an example. Let's say you grew up with "white glove" service being what you experienced in life. However, the person you are asking to provide that level of service today grew up in a "latex glove" environment, meaning they never experienced the level of service you're expecting. As a result, your metaphor doesn't connect, and that is where the problem lies.

Another example is the phrase "blue-ribbon service." If you were raised in a generation that experienced county fairs, there was only one blue ribbon awarded in each category. Because of that, the phrase "blue-ribbon service" makes sense. If you're talking to a Millennial, everybody got a blue ribbon, even those who came in 15th! This reference doesn't land at all with this age group and makes it difficult for them to understand your messaging.

Commitment. If you signed on with a company as an employee in your 20s and you're planning to stay for 10 to 20 years, you're building social capital in that organization. You're creating and maintaining relationships with other people, so it causes you to make different choices in behavior, and that affects how you deliver

customer service. If I am planning on being at an organization only for a short time, I don't see myself as part of a community. It's more of a transactional experience: my time in exchange for money. This mindset may influence how motivated I am to serve the customer. If I am going to be here only a few months, I won't have the same level of commitment I would if I planned to stay for years.

Compassion. Anna says that compassion for another's experience is the magic to service. Consideration for another person's formative experiences is the secret sauce in making people flock to you as well.

As role models, we like to think that we taught compassion to the younger generations. But, in reality, we were so focused on making them feel special that we didn't teach as much compassion as we could have, and now we're dealing with the outcomes. As an organization, go back to what you might think are rudimentary skills.

> ...compassion for another's experience is the magic to service.

We didn't require our children to understand others, and now in our customer-service training we have to do some basic work. It starts with understanding the generational experience of each employee so they can help understand the experience of the others.

I think it all comes down to a simple thought: If a leader believes that good service should be obvious to everyone, then he or she does not understand Generational CODES.

(To learn more about Anna Liotta and her many resources on generations, visit www.AnnaLiotta.com.)

2. Ignoring the currency factor

Everyone has a currency—that which causes them to behave in a certain way. For a lot of people, money is their currency. Money is what talks. But interestingly, there are many other motivators, such as knowledge, power, being included, an important title, or

flexibility in the work schedule. That may be the reason your part-time staff is satisfied with their job: because it provides the luxury of flexible hours or a shift time that meets their family obligations.

Sometimes figuring out what someone's currency is can be hard. For Ellie, it wasn't necessarily the light bulb itself, but the control she had over deciding when to comply. When the consequence outweighed the need to win the battle, she changed her behavior.

Each of your team members has a currency. Once you figure out what it is, a modified version of the Ellie story comes into play. For example, during my career there was a time when I managed a front-desk team. There was one person who had a commitment as a mother every Tuesday afternoon at 4 p.m. that was important to her, so I made arrangements for her schedule to release her from duty two hours early without pay. She was thrilled, as it allowed her to do the activity with her child and not have to take all her vacation time to do it. However, after a few months of this privilege, she started to come in to work a few minutes late on many days. Those few minutes turned into a length of time that was noticeable and an inconvenience to her co-workers. When I met with her, instead of just asking her to please be sure to come to work on time (a technique that seems to rarely work in this instance), I instead went straight for her currency to gain compliance. In this case, her currency was flexibility of the Tuesday hours. So I said something like, "Sophie, I was able to move things around in order to accommodate your desire for an early out on Tuesdays. However, if you are not able to punch in on time every day and be at your station ready to take care of patients, then I will have no choice but to put you back on the schedule until 5 p.m. on Tuesdays." I never had to ask again. This time I went straight for the light bulb and saved us all a lot of stress and outbursts.

Generational differences often play a big role in determining an employee's currency. As shared earlier in this book, I believe that praise is the gasoline between paychecks. An organization needs to have something other than money that makes people stay engaged,

something that causes them to stand up slightly taller and to go home a little happier. Praise is one of the pieces, but you have to have a clear understanding what each person's gasoline is in life.

Anna believes that a Millennial's gasoline is a combination of praise and purpose. It can't be just praise, because when you get too much of a certain thing, you don't have respect for it. Laying on a pile of false praise ends up looking like a trophy for everything. We saw Millennials pack up boxes full of trophies and ribbons with a "so what" attitude: "I've got a bunch of these, so who cares?" In addition to the kudos, there is a need to have consistent feedback, and Millennials get really frustrated when you think that all they need is flowery attaboys. What they would prefer is that mix between praise and the context that what they're doing is purposeful in the world.

> "...a Millennial's gasoline is a combination of praise and purpose."

I challenge you to consider another word we could add to that phrase: praise, purpose, and an opportunity. Millennials are looking for opportunities and they're looking for access. *Do you give me a chance to rise? Because I desire to climb.* If you aren't creating those opportunities, then as an employer you are transactional in their lives. You are not a destination, you are a milestone at best, a moment in their journey.

Each person is an individual and, as a leader, the only way you're going to learn about their currency or gasoline is to spend some time with them. If you are the CEO of a large company, obviously you are not going to connect with every person, but there should be an expectation placed on the department managers to foster rapport and have a clear understanding of the staff needs. It is critical that staff not feel isolated and unheard, no matter how large the company.

If leaders do not engage their hearts, their minds, and their spirits, they run the risk of having a disengaged employee.

3. Diverging values

When the goals, actions, and values of management don't align with those of the team, divergence begins. A gap in the goals leads to retention failure. Often leaders will give the message "Hey, here is what we are all about. Either get on board the train or get off." I don't think we spend enough time thinking about goal alignment and striving to keep the paths in sync, like two vertical lines that mirror one another. For example, when I started my corporate job at the eye facility, I was so aligned with everything management did that my "personal path" (meaning goals, actions, and values) was exactly the same, running parallel like the double lines on a highway. When the organization was at the peak of growth, I was given the opportunity to step up to a mid-level management position, which eventually led to the top level of administration. This title allowed me access to more data, confidential meetings, and internal challenges. With that knowledge, my commitment to some of the choices wavered a bit and my vertical line began to drift away from center.

As the years passed, the trajectory of the lines continued until the gap between the two was too large to sustain. The original owners had begun an exit strategy from the practice, and part of that process was to sell the clinic and surgery center to our local hospital. While the hospital is a fine institution, they did not have the same vertical line when it came to marketing or liaison work with our referral sources. It became obvious to me early during the transition that I would not be able to stay if I wanted to maintain my own values. Eventually I formed my own exit strategy and left my employment under great terms.

To retain your staff, be aware of the areas where the gap can be narrowed. One the best ways to do that is to see knowledge as power. Provide as much internal information as possible through staff meetings, personal coaching, or employment reviews. Having the confidence to be as transparent as possible helps staff feel connected and truly part of the family. Obviously, some data must remain confidential in any business setting, but beware of how much "in the dark" time your staff is expected to accept.

One time, I did some consultation work with a privately-owned small clinic. The doctor had decided to expand his practice by moving to a new building that was a major step up in curb appeal. He confided all the details with me but refused to tell his staff, for reasons I am still not sure about. I encouraged him to at least "prime the pump" by letting them know he was thinking about it, although the contract was not signed and the deal could still fall through. He did not agree. Several days after this conversation, his commercial real estate agent faxed paperwork regarding the sale directly to the office line. Within moments, the entire staff found out about the move, and most felt excluded and unimportant. The team eventually did move to the new digs, but I am not sure they ever got back that same cohesive team feel they once had. This is a perfect example of my point. He could have kept them in the loop as trusted "family" while keeping the details of the purchase limited to him and his partner. Today, I believe if I asked, he would tell me that things changed when they grew—that having more square footage, more offerings, and increased staff led to a difference in the culture. While all of that may be true, the biggest change came when he stopped treating his original team like the tight work family they thought they were. Today, most of them work elsewhere.

4. Not meeting basic needs

During my years of consulting with small businesses on customer service and staff-development issues, I would conduct one-on-one interviews with each team member to learn more about the internal health of the business. When a boss received outstanding comments regarding his or her leadership, I asked this simple question: "What does your boss do that prompts this glorious praise from you?" The answer always fell into the category of caring about them as a person, not just about the role they filled at work.

By paying attention to more than just the bottom line, stronger relationships can be built. Consider offering healthy-living programs or giving time off when needed without making the staff member feel guilty. Pay attention to what their physical comfort needs are in the

workplace. I once interviewed a disgruntled employee at the request of her employer because he could not figure out what was causing the change in her attitude over the previous few months. It only took a little prodding to find out she was extremely uncomfortable in her desk chair and had asked him repeatedly for months if the worn-out chair could be replaced. According to her, the request was always met with "Let me think about it," and then nothing ever happened. Such an easy solution, but because he was procrastinating on a small decision, she interpreted it as a lack of caring. It makes sense that happier employees will stick when their needs are being met and they feel valued.

Simple Facts on Retention

Retaining talent that is already trained and on board with your organization's service mindset is much easier than hiring new staff. If you make it a priority to learn what motivates your team and help them understand your service expectations, your employees will be satisfied, and they'll stay with you longer. And that's a fact.

Discussion Questions

How do the Generational CODES™ show up in your current leadership challenges?

What specific training and mentoring tools are in place to help team members succeed?

Is there a gap between the goals of leadership and the commitment of the team?

Do you know the currency of each of your team members?

Can you identify your own currency?

Creating an Extraordinary Guest Encounter System:
Pulling It All Together

The phrase "secret sauce" appears in the urban dictionary as a term created by Jack in the Box restaurants to refer to the condiment similar to Thousand Island dressing that they added to their burgers. In the 1980s, the company thought the phrase was a way to differentiate itself from other fast-food chains. In business, "secret sauce" has come to mean that special something that makes one product, service, or company stand out from everyone else. *Why do some places seem to have the secret sauce while others fall short? How does one use that extra-special small change to gain an edge on the competition?*

The Winner Is Chosen by the Palate Preference of the Judge

What makes you choose one thing over another? It's usually something small and subtle, like an individual ingredient that makes one recipe for chocolate-chip cookies out of this world and another just so-so. There must be 100 different versions of the popular American dessert. The classic recipe is even found on the back of the famous yellow bag of Nestle® Toll House® chocolate chips. But, add just a pinch of a single ingredient or switch from butter to margarine, and you get a totally different result.

My family has a tradition that has been in place my entire life. Every year, on the weekend after Labor Day, we attend our county fair, where we get the chance to step back in time. We do odd things by today's standards, like buy raffle tickets for a live pig (which will be

packaged for your freezer the next week), eat corny dogs (always accompanied with a lemon shake-up), and admire the handiwork of those who can craft, cook, or can. I clearly remember about 15 years ago when my husband entered our delicious chocolate-chip cookies in one of the fair's many competitions. We don't use any special ingredients. Instead, the *preparation* is his confidential weapon. Our secret is that the cookies are hand-mixed until they're super creamy—no electric mixer.

On the first day of the fair that year, we raced straight to the building where the judging took place and peeked in the display case. We strained our eyes to identify the blue-ribbon winner in the chocolate-chip cookie category, then wondered what made *those* cookies award-worthy. Why were they better than the delicious ones we entered that only earned second place? Both cookies might be fantastic-tasting, totally acceptable treats to serve company, but the judge is asked to pick only *one*.

It's the same way your customer ultimately chooses which company earns his dollar. The winner is usually the one that has a pinch of something special, a single ingredient or a process that wins them over—the secret sauce.

My search for mastering the secret of secret sauce began during my career at the Hauser-Ross Eye Institute. We were known for our amazing customer service, and eventually word got out that we had a secret of some kind. As we grew and became well-known in our community, other industries started calling to ask if I could come and share a glimpse behind the curtain. The first call came from a local bank, and my initial reaction was to pass, since I had no idea how the banking world works on the inside. But soon I learned that it didn't matter what the industry is, because we all have one thing in common: *people*. We share the same challenges in developing stellar staff and we share the same goal of trying to keep customers happy and coming back.

Thus started my two decades of the study of people. What behaviors allow staff to thrive and strive for more? I studied what specific things companies did to be noteworthy and successful in a world where customers have seemingly infinite options for spending their discretionary income.

Creating an Extraordinary Guest Encounter System

I am intrigued with why some businesses explode while others implode. Is it because of poor leadership? Sometimes, but not always. Is it because they don't have a solid training system that gets all team members on the same page? Often, but not always. Is it because they didn't do enough market research or keep a close enough ear to the ground to determine where their weak spots are? Maybe.

What I do know for sure is this: That which is measured tends to improve. If an organization doesn't analyze its situation routinely and accurately, trouble will surface. There are so many moving parts in a business. Market pull, finicky buyers, difficult staff, challenge of turnover, inconsistent training, ineffective leadership, and shrinking profit margins are just a few examples of what we must face daily when running a business. It's because of these challenges that I developed The Guest Encounter™, a virtual training tool to help everyone get on the same page and hopefully create a winning recipe for their organization.

The Guest Encounter

Every time your team has an encounter with a "guest"—a customer, client, patient, or patron—it's a snapshot in time. It reminds me of a picture I once saw taken from inside a vehicle going through a car wash. The sun was streaming through the windshield in a way that caused the light to refract and create a rainbow of beautiful shades of turquoise, green, and pink across the glass. Mixed with the soap and water, it created a picture so pretty it was almost frame-worthy. However, 30 seconds later, it no longer looked anything like that. The car moved farther down the track, the angle of the sun changed, and, in an instant, the view from inside was clouded with filthy, ugly water. Both snapshots are accurate and the time lapse between them is less than 30 seconds. But the environment and the feeling toward the experience are totally different. That's the same thing that happens when your guest encounters a member of your team.

When the guest moves from one team member to the next at the same visit through the transfer of a phone call or a transition to a different department, it's like the car moving along the car-wash track. Each new encounter can create a different impression. Is the

experience better than the first moment or less impressive? Either way, it can ultimately change the way the customer feels about the whole visit.

Another important group of people who are often overlooked in the training process are the internal customers we discussed in a previous chapter. Simply put, these are the people who stand next to you daily working to deliver the expected product or service to your end user. Because many times your work relationships begin to take on a family dynamic, it can sometimes get dicey. Familiarity of your conversations, tolerance of questionable behaviors, eroding respect, favoritism and team alliances are just a few of the challenging situations that can present themselves over time. It's very important as you process the content of this book that focuses mainly on external customers that you take the time to keep your internal guest in mind as well.

> If you aren't serving our customers, you better be serving someone who is.

My boss used to say, "If you aren't serving our customers, you better be serving someone who is." What he meant was that every task being done in the organization must tie into a path that eventually feeds into our guest interactions. Not every team member will have direct contact with an end user, but undoubtedly, the work they are doing plays a role in the final delivery to the buyer. At the very least, their level of engagement in the organization matters. Engagement is where service starts. Although these encounters happen dozens of times each day, many organizations have not given a lot of thought to the small things their team might be doing, internally and externally, to tip the experience to the negative, or the many, many easy things they can do to tilt the guests' opinions to the positive. That's what the Guest Encounter process is all about—identifying and implementing the best customer experience at your address.

One way to pull all of the puzzle pieces of this book together into a complete picture is with a contextual model. I first learned about this process from leadership expert Neen James, MBA. She helped

me take the somewhat-random ideas that I had collected over the years and put them into a system. According to Neen, "Contextual models really appeal to the strategic thinkers of your organization, and they also help provide a framework for the very tactical people on your team."

As she was teaching me this concept, I was uncertain exactly how it would impact my work, but I trusted her brilliance and leaned in to it 100%. After several modifications for clarity, I eventually incorporated it into the content of my customer-service keynote called *The 10¢ Decision.* It was instantly clear that my newly devised contextual model helped snap the pieces of advice into an organized approach to improving customer service.

6 Steps to Achieving an Extraordinary Guest Encounter

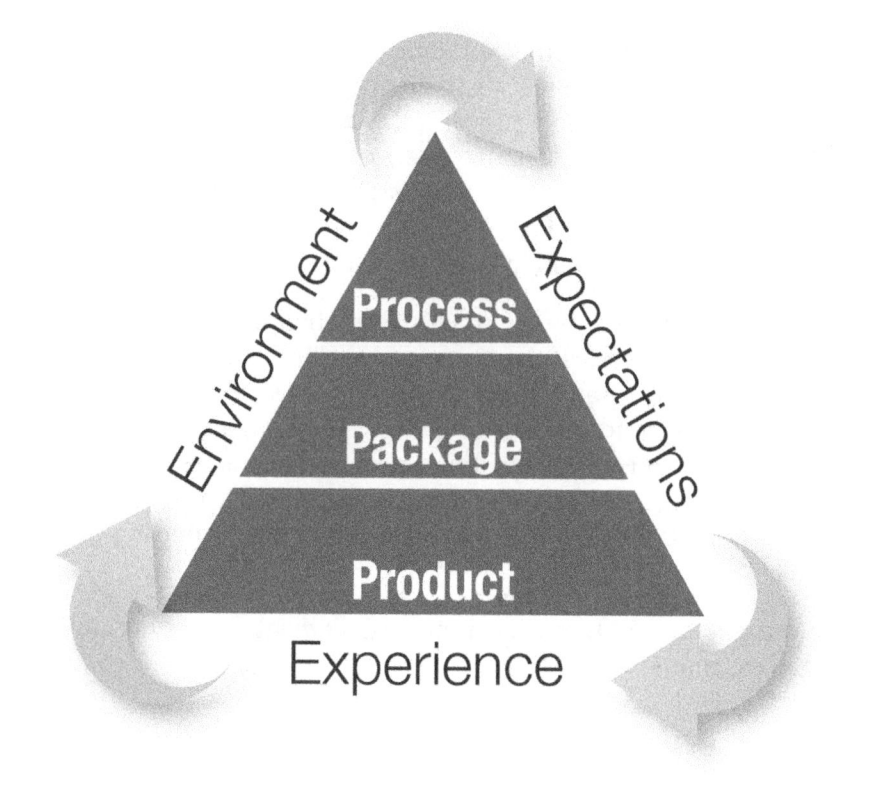

Creating an Extraordinary Guest Encounter System

1. Product

Whatever your core service or product is, it must meet or exceed the needs of the buyer. Of course we know many components go into a product's success, including cost, quality, ease of use, and urgency of need. Most consumers would not consider fast food the best culinary quality, but it meets the needs of speed, low cost, and standardization. Ask yourself if your product or service is the very best it can be for your business objectives.

For example, we have a favorite pizza place in our community that is family owned and not part of a national chain. We were loyal customers for years, never ordering pizza from anyone else. Several years ago, we took out-of-town guests there for a fun evening and the pizza was terrible. We looked around and noticed many of the other tables were leaving a majority of their pie untouched. After inquiring why the taste was different, our server shared that the owner had decided to try a new brand of cheese. I'm making the assumption that the switch may have been made to keep costs down, but I don't know that for sure. We stopped going. Rumor has it they have changed back to their original cheese brand, but we have already started being loyal followers of another restaurant. I call this the "bad bowl of soup syndrome," meaning that even loyal customers will quit coming over one bad experience. Sometimes without warning, they leave your buying cycle, never letting you know why or giving you a chance to make it right.

Although staff often have no control over changing or improving the core product or service, they are on the frontlines, where they can pay attention to small details that matter. It's very important that they watch for trends in consumption so they can alert management when something is off. If the daily special entrée is frequently being sent back to the kitchen, the servers may need to alert someone about a potential problem. Awareness is key when spotting product issues.

Are you satisfied with your current product quality, or is this an issue that needs more scrutiny?

2. Package

What a product or service is called makes a difference, and the "package" it comes in matters even more. Now is the time to do a quick review to see if an upgrade is possible at a very low cost.

I know of a spa that offered a treatment package that included a deep-tissue massage, mud bath, and seaweed wrap. Sounds delightful, right? It was called the "#2 Package." Not so delightful. After a little creative brainstorming, they decided that since their location was decorated in moons and stars, they could name their packages in a more desirable way based on their motif. They renamed #2 "The Celestial Moment." Now that's something I'd pay $200 for! Be on the lookout for great examples of this in famous brands.

Be sure to review the chapter titled "Packaging That Gets Noticed: Get Creative to Better Position Your Product."

Do you have anything that could be repackaged or renamed in your organization to create a bigger impact?

3. Process

The series of steps that it takes to complete an action needs to be smooth, simple, and succinct. This is true for our end user as well as the internal team. So much waste can be found in paper usage, labor hours, and unnecessary tasks. Most often when I push back on processes or rules that have no obvious purpose, the response I get is "But that's the way it has always been done."

For example, a healthcare client had patients fill out the registration form from scratch every year. This form included the typical questions we expect to answer, like address, phone, and insurance. Plus, the second page was filled with a complete medical-history questionnaire including past surgeries and family history. These are all things that could easily change during the course of a year. But it also had a lot of spaces to fill in data that will never change for a patient, like birth date and Social Security number. When established patients asked about the extra step, the response was a valid one: "We want to make sure you have given us any changes that may have occurred since we last saw you."

It would make more sense if they printed out the current version of the most recent form and asked the patient to review it for accuracy,

marking changes or additions where appropriate, and having a space at the bottom of each page for the patient to sign and date that the medical record was reviewed. This would be way less hassle for the patient and would speed up the process time in reception. Before implementing any idea like this, it is imperative that you check with the "powers that be" in your industry to make sure your change is ethical, legal, and appropriate. I know of great ideas that caused unexpected problems because the research was skipped.

In other situations, a simple change that comes without risk can be made by the staff.

For example, it's standard that first-class airline travelers are offered a beverage before takeoff. The flight attendants have no control over the brand or the quality of the taste. However, they do have control over when the beverage is presented. Sometimes they offer it first thing after a passenger sits down, allowing time to enjoy it while the plane finishes loading. Other attendants will wait until the cabin door is closed to serve, causing passengers to either chug it quickly or pass on it altogether.

What processes do you have in place that are antiquated or in need of a deep analysis?

The second half of the contextual model, illustrated by the arrows on the outside of the pyramid, comes with two layers. "People" are defined as your customers and your staff members. It is vital to identify the expectations, experiences, and environment that matter for *both* groups.

4. Expectations
Expectations of the Customer
When it comes to our customers or guests, we need to set a proper expectation of what the encounter will be like for them. A real estate agent who has all of the transaction steps written out and explained in advance will have clients who are less stressed and more likely to be satisfied because they know what to expect. It doesn't matter if we are talking construction, healthcare, retail, or tourism, everything goes more smoothly when things are spelled out and carried out according to plan.

Creating an Extraordinary Guest Encounter System

Expectations of the Staff

To handle the expectations of your staff, you need to create proper boundaries of performance. Establishing your service culture and making sure that an appropriate level of time is spent training and maintaining standards makes all the difference. An expectation that all staff live by the "BIS" rule at all times is a simple example. BIS stands for "butt in seat"—the time of day that each employee is expected to be at their work station punched in, groomed, already finished with their most recent meal, and ready to perform their daily tasks. On a regular basis, I have leaders tell me about staff members who roll in 15 minutes late, still putting on makeup or knotting a tie while toasting a bagel and brewing their K-Cup® of coffee, all while delaying the workflow. It's very frustrating that the simple task of getting to work on time can be challenging for so many people. Solution? Be clear about the expectations and consequences for non-compliance. Then, as hard as it may be, managers must follow through with repercussions for habitually late employees.

> **To handle the expectations, you need to create proper boundaries of performance.**

Have you set proper expectations for guests and staff?

5. Experience

Experience of the Customer

Experience is the personal engagement during the encounter. Creating an exchange that is so pleasant it's worth talking about afterward is obviously the key to word-of-mouth advertising. It's amazing to me how a few simple 10¢ decisions can tip an experience into the noteworthy category.

We had a large addition put on our home years ago. I reached out to four contractors who specialize in remodeling. Two never showed up for the first appointment, one kept the appointment but never followed up with a proposal, and the fourth one pulled into our driveway exactly at 2 p.m., the scheduled time for our first appointment, and he was a perfect professional. Not only did he stay on budget, but the communication was outstanding throughout the four-month process. He and his team did everything that I teach

in this book and maybe even a few things more. When the job was over, we became one of his favorite testimonials. Whenever he had a new client who wanted to peek at his work, he would call and ask permission to send the prospective client over to check out our addition. Not only were we happy to invite them in, but we would sing his praises to anyone who would listen. Could someone else have done the work? Yes, of course. But I don't believe there is anyone who could have made our overall experience better. It's been about 15 years since we did this project, and now we are in need of this type of service again to prepare our home to sell. There was never a doubt whom we would call. We didn't do a price comparison, we didn't check to see who else is now in the marketplace, we didn't ask friends for their thoughts. I picked up the phone and called Ken Spears Construction.

Experience of the Staff

When I interviewed candidates for a job opening at our organization, I would usually ask about their experience at their previous place of employment. Many times they told tales of being treated poorly, hence the job search. I once asked an applicant if she could give me a specific example of something that had prompted her to look for a new job. She shared how her current boss yelled at everyone in front of customers and that the overall treatment of co-workers left her feeling hurt and underappreciated. Those answers were valid concerns, and I explained that we made it our mission not to allow any staff member to have an experience like that while a part of our team. I agreed to hire her and she remained a committed employee for many years, telling me many times that the experiences were night-and-day different.

Employee engagement is the foundation of delivering great service.

Can you brag that you provide the same level of attention to the experience of your team as you do to the experience of your customer?

6. Environment
Environment for the Customer

The environment is defined as the surroundings or conditions of the place of business. Low-cost decisions like keeping the square footage neat and clean is a given, but I'm shocked at the number of times

this simple concept is overlooked. Get a new perspective by taking a walk around your business as if you have never seen it before. Park where you customers park, use the same entrance, look, smell, listen, and taste if applicable.

I once had a business meeting with a doctor who was interested in hiring me for some staff-development consulting work. When I arrived at her office, I spotted a funny sign taped to the wall behind the receptionist desk. It read, "I go from zero to bitch in .7 seconds." Although funny, it was highly inappropriate for it to be within the patient's view. Later, when I met with the doctor privately, I asked about the sign. And what do you think she said? That's right, she said, "What sign?" On further review, we found out the sign was printed and posted by a staff member weeks before, but because the doctor never saw the reception area and front desk from the patient's point of view, she was unaware that it existed.

Make sure the overall feel of your environment provides customers with the best impression by keeping a line item in your budget for periodically updating your interior design, or at the very least committing to small touch-ups when needed.

Obviously, a brick-and-mortar business is the first thing that comes to mind when we think of environment, but online businesses need to pay big attention to the digital environment as well. Not long ago, I had a customer-service issue that required an email correspondence with a travel company regarding a gift certificate. Instead of a digital environment that said "friendly and helpful," I received a very rude email that said only four words, "That certificate is expired." They didn't even attempt to create an engaged encounter or save me as a customer.

Environment for the Staff
What about the environment you create for your team in the workplace? Do they feel safe, cared for, relevant, respected, and able to enjoy the work you do together? I've had the privilege of being behind the scenes of hundreds of businesses over my career, and I can see which ones are "rockin' and rollin'" as a unit almost immediately. And although I have never done an actual study of the attributes of the winning teams, I truly believe it comes down to the

genuine caring, compassion, and family-like environment created by leadership. When the customer is treated right, the staff are valued, and the products and services are something they are proud to represent, the work is much easier.

Contentment is a strong word and a goal all of us as leaders should aspire to achieve for ourselves and our staff. A state of satisfaction and overall peaceful happiness sounds just delightful, doesn't it? The big question is what does it take to achieve that in a business where you have influence?

The one leader who comes to my mind when I think "environment setter" owns a medical clinic where every employee told me the same thing during our one-on-one pre-event interviews. Although each used words unique to their personality, it all translated to the same core message. The owner of the clinic came in every day on time with a consistent attitude of positivity. He spoke kindly, showed interest in their personal lives, and allowed outside priorities to carry as much importance as their work duties. He shared the wealth when it was a good harvest and shared the concerns when numbers were down. He created a family environment with room for fun and laughter while still maintaining a professional atmosphere. I'm sure it's no surprise that he has very little turnover, loves his job, rarely has drama to deal with, and is at a very comfortable income level. It seems to me that the environment he has created over the past 30 years is the logical reason why he is successful and why he and his team are content.

In what ways have you and your management team worked to create an environment of contentment not only for your customers, but also for your valuable team?

I think we likely agree that customer service is often common sense. However, if we leave common sense to chance, there is the possibility it fails in execution. The good news is that the steps outlined in this book are easy to accomplish. All it takes is focus and effort from you and your team. Instead of getting stuck on the major changes you could make, I encourage you to start with a simple thing you can do—*The 10¢ Decision*—and prove to yourself how small change pays off big.

Creating an Extraordinary Guest Encounter System

Discussion Questions

What part of the triangular contextual model is your organization currently excelling at?

What part of the system needs the most attention right now?

Which part of the triad (customers, leaders, staff) is not getting enough of their needs met at this time?

What can you gain by reading this book from the other direction?

If you choose not to read it, why would that be?

Epilogue

Dear Leaders,

I encourage you to honestly self-assess your ability to offer the things I've described in this book. If you have dysfunctional staff members you are struggling to manage day-to-day, it may be time to invest in leadership training or coaching. Changing culture is one of the hardest things to do, and getting help can make all the difference in the outcome.

Please take the time to flip over the book and read it from the other side.

A very small portion of the text is duplicated, so there are many more ideas in the other half. Plus, to achieve desired results from the people who work for you, you must think about their challenges and see things through their goggles as well. I am confident it will be worth your time and effort in order to pull all of this together.

Final Thought

I had the privilege of working for years under the mentorship of many doctors and a stellar management team. It is through their unrelenting training that my entire professional career was formed. Providing superior customer service was so important to me that I, in turn, was asked to begin teaching others our secrets. I didn't know at the time that it would become my life's work as a professional speaker and trainer. There isn't a topic I feel as much passion about as I do service.

Please remember that every customer, client, patient, or patron comes to you needing something. If we can fulfill that need and treat them like a treasured guest in our home, then every encounter can go beyond expectations. Not because it cost a fortune to deliver the best, but because you were bold enough to repeatedly make 10¢ decisions.

Flip Time!